Loose Him
― AND ―
Let Him Go!

Loose Him
— and —
Let Him Go!
Deliverance and Spiritual Growth

Dr. Moussa Toure

Pleasant W rd
A Division of WINEPRESS PUBLISHING

© 2007 by Moussa Touré. All rights reserved.

Pleasant Word (a division of WinePress Publishing, PO Box 428, Enumclaw, WA 98022) functions only as book publisher. As such, the ultimate design, content, editorial accuracy, and views expressed or implied in this work are those of the author.

No part of this publication may be reproduced, stored in a retrieval system or transmitted in any way by any means—electronic, mechanical, photocopy, recording or otherwise—without the prior permission of the copyright holder, except as provided by USA copyright law.

Unless otherwise noted, all Scriptures are taken from the King James Version of the Bible.

Scripture references marked NASB are taken from the New American Standard Bible, © 1960, 1963, 1968, 1971, 1972, 1973, 1975, 1977 by The Lockman Foundation. Used by permission.

ISBN 13: 978-1-4141-0846-9
ISBN 10: 1-4141-0846-X
Library of Congress Catalog Card Number: 2006908180

Dedication

To those among us who are suffering oppression: May you see the deliverance of the Lord.

To my spiritual father and mentor, Bishop D. G. Johnson, whose transformational teaching and visionary leadership nurtured, guided, and equipped me for the work of ministry.

To my Bethel pastoral teams, church leadership, and members: Your partnership has encouraged and helped me develop the deliverance ministry.

To the prayer, deliverance, and evangelism ministry: Your prayers have helped me walk under the leading and the power of the Holy Spirit.

TABLE OF CONTENTS

Foreword xi
Acknowledgments xv
Background xvii
Introduction xix

Chapter One: Biblical Foundation for Deliverance 25
    Deliverance Is a Covenant Right 25
    Place and Role of Deliverance in the
        Christian's Spiritual Life 29
    The Role of the Church in Deliverance 44

Chapter Two: Understanding Deliverance 55
    Definition of Deliverance 55
        Explanation of the Hebrew/Greek Term 55
    Deliverance Is a Continual Process 56
    Purpose of Deliverance 58
    The Temple of the Holy Ghost 65
    Questionnaire 68

Chapter Three: Dependence upon the Holy Spirit......... 73
   An Inner Familiarity with the Word of God............ 73
   A Life of Prayer and Fasting....................... 76
   The Responsibility of the Minister of God............... 81
   Questionnaire...................................... 83

Chapter Four: Identifying Demons............................ 87
   Operating in Spiritual Gifts to Discern the Symptoms of Demonic Presence 88
   Knowing the Word of God Concerning Satan and His Demons... 89
   Understanding Practical Spiritual Doors 103
   Understanding Other Practical Doors.................... 105
   Spiritual Bondage (as a Result of Spiritual Doors)....................... 111
   Questionnaire.. 121

Chapter Five: Casting Out Demons............................. 125
   Preparation for God's Intervention 125
   Execution of Deliverance 129

Chapter Six: The Renewal of the Mind....................... 137
   Self-Deliverance After Deliverance....................... 139
   Conclusion 139
   Questionnaire... 140

Appendix 1: Four-Step Session for Deliverance............ 143

Appendix 2: Deliverance Prayer to Set the Oppressed Free 147
   Preparation of Spiritual Atmosphere..................... 147
   Deliverance Prayer.................................... 148

Appendix 3: Prayer to Bring Healing to the Sick 153
   Begin with the Blood of Jesus.......................... 153

Continue by Praying for the Intervention
of the Holy Spirit 155
Continue Praying to Cast Out Evil Spirits
and Heal Sicknesses 156

Appendix 4: Activating Covenant Prayer 157

Appendix 5: Soul Diagnosis Form 159
Family-Level Doorways and Generational Curses
(Exodus 20:3–5) 161
Recommendations for Preparation before Deliverance
Session 176

Appendix 6: Hebrew/Greek Terms Translated
by the English Verb Deliver 177

Appendix 7: Bibliography 179

Foreword

I am honored to be asked to write this foreword; I am also proud. Honored because the Lord will use this book to set many people free; proud because the author is my spiritual son. And any father would be proud of a son who has done a magnificent job with something as important as this: a book on spiritual warfare and deliverance.

All who desire to see God's people free and believers strong and vibrant will benefit immensely from Dr. Touré's work. It provides both theological and practical help for the individual or church that wants to remove one of the major obstacles to spiritual growth: demonic oppression. Dr. Touré calls that "preparing the soil" so that the Word can take root and produce fruit.

Believers across this nation and around the world are overwhelmed, oppressed, struggling, and defeated in their attempt to live the abundant life Christ came to give them. I am convinced, however, that if more churches would embrace the ministry of deliverance and employ a systematic approach as suggested in offering deliverance to those in need the results would be phenomenal. Instead of an army of weak and ineffective believers, a new generation of bold conquerors would arise, set free by God and empowered to set others free.

Dr. Touré is on a mission to raise up such an army that can enforce Satan's defeat. And this book, *"Loose Him and Let Him Go,"* is a weapon he has released against the prince of darkness. As a manual, it will multiply exponentially the number of churches and believers equipped to set the captives free. With a significantly increased army of deliverance ministers unleashed, Satan's ploy to keep people, especially born-again believers, bound and ineffective, is in serious trouble.

Not everyone can write a book, and only a very few have the combination of intellect and experience to write a practical manual on the subject of deliverance. Dr. Touré is one of the few. Holding several masters degrees in the sciences and a PhD in theology, he is intellectually prepared to analyze the problems, research the issues, and address the controversies that unfortunately surround and hinder the ministry of deliverance.

Even more importantly, however, Dr. Touré writes from the vantage point of one who is personally engaged in the ministry of deliverance. His firsthand and ongoing ministry in helping people find freedom in Christ means that the information shared here is not mere theory or speculation.

No, these truths are tried and proven, and they are included here because they work! I urge you to take advantage of the wealth of knowledge and experience found here. But don't keep it to yourself and don't read this just for

Foreword

information! Learn, practice, and then pass it on! What this manual teaches, when practiced by you or your church, will revolutionize your ministry and incapacitate the enemy.

RT. REV. DR. DARLINGSTON G. JOHNSON
Presiding Prelate, BWOMI

Acknowledgments

This achievement is the result of the work of many who contributed in various measures. I am grateful to you all who have through prayers and other ways provided input to make this work a reality.

To my wife, Esther, for your love, prayers, wisdom, and faithfulness that allow me to give myself completely to Him.

To Yannick and Faith, our two wonderful gifts of the Lord who make me feel the joy and this refreshment that can only come from your children.

To Laurentine Batonga for your trust, encouragement, and help. You ceased not to push me toward the completion of the work and guiding the team in order to bring forth the final product.

Finally, to Esther Eyere for her assistance in editing this book. I am ever grateful.

Background

After his post master degree in aviation and three master degrees in physics, computer science, and finance, Reverend M. Touré pursued his career as an administrator of civil aviation in France and then at the World Bank in Washington, DC in the United States. In 1989, during a one-week trip to his home country, Burkina Faso, the Lord Jesus appeared to him and spoke to him, and at that very moment, the old M. Touré "died" and a new man was born as a result of this encounter with the Lord.

Even though he is from a Muslim background, he is now a servant of Jehovah God (Father, Son, Holy Spirit), whose Son, Jesus, shed His blood at Calvary for the remission of sin, gave His life, and rose the third day from the dead.

Over the years, his passion for Jesus and his commitment to the Word of God and to the work of the Holy Spirit have grown stronger. Through the leadership and mentoring of Bishop Darlingston Johnson, his pastor since 1992 and leader of Bethel World Outreach Ministries (a network of two hundred churches with headquarters based in Silver

Spring, Maryland, in the United Sates), Rev. M. Touré has learned and been trained to walk with the Lord in prayer, in obedience to the Word of God, in winning souls, in deliverance, and in making disciples. In addition, he also spent three years studying at the Bethel Bible Institute. He became, in 1994, deacon in charge of the Prayer, Deliverance, and Evangelism Ministry. In 1997, he became assistant pastor to the bishop for the same ministry and was ordained as a minister of the gospel of our Lord Jesus Christ in 2001.

After traveling for many years to over thirty countries in Europe, Asia, the Caribbean, Africa, and North America, spreading the Good News of salvation through Jesus Christ, Rev. M. Touré is now a messenger that the Lord has prepared for the nations for these end times. He is author of "The Prayer Warrior's Confession," a document to help believers "hold fast 'their' profession." Rev. Moussa Touré is married to Esther, a woman of prayer and founder of "The Watchmen on the Wall Ministry—Prayer Houses for Nations." The Lord has blessed them with two wonderful children, Yannick and Faith Anna Deborah.

Introduction

Many Christians know that they should read the Word of God and apply it to their lives to make it a part of them. Many want to pray in order to develop their relationship with the Lord. Most of them want to be used by God, and some strongly believe that the Lord has called them for a particular work, even in His Church, maybe even in one of the fivefold ministries. However, one basic problem is that many are discouraged in their efforts by hindrances and do not know how to break through these obstacles. The second nature of the problem is that those who want to help may not be able to provide the appropriate intervention needed in terms of deliverance.

Deliverance is a means by which one escapes the oppression of the enemy. Spiritual deliverance is an action through which God drives out a spirit being from the life of a victim and sets him free from bondage or captivity by breaking spiritual ties and putting an end to satanic actions and curses.

Yet, who says deliverance means possession by demonic spirits? From there, voices start to arise by those who are against the ministry of deliverance. The strongest belief against a Christian having a demon is the impossibility for the Holy Spirit and a demon indwelling the same body. This belief is not biblical (as we will see in Part 1 of this book) neither logical.

It is not possible to prove that there is or has been a Christian who has never been inhabited by a demon. These past years, we have delivered many Christians from satanic and demonic oppression. Many others are delivered every day in our ministry.

Every oppressed person needs to know that no case is hopeless. No matter what the devil has done, Jesus is willing and able to set His people free just as He did when He was on Earth. That is why the Church must not dismiss or neglect the ministry of deliverance. To do so is perilous:

- It denies to those who have been invaded by the enemy the understanding and help they so desperately need.
- It does not warn those who are not oppressed of the peril of being invaded by evil spirits; nor does it warn of what will happen if they fail to hold onto who they are in Christ and backslide into willful sin.
- It brings opposition to those ministering deliverance and even accusation of using "Beelzebub's" power.

The ministry of deliverance is also one of the means by which the saints can be developed spiritually. However, in making disciples, it is one of the most overlooked. The general assumption in the body of Christ concerning discipleship is that all saints can, by themselves, through regular

INTRODUCTION

church meetings and activities, get to the point where the Word of God is working in their lives. Such understanding has prevented the local church from organizing deliverance ministry as an integral part of the discipleship process in the Church. But experience has proven that spiritual growth and the process of discipleship can be facilitated for the new convert and many of those struggling in their Christian walk when the ministry of deliverance is included in the spiritual growth process.

Unfortunately, many people in churches today and even some ministers do not want to have anything to do with the deliverance ministry. They use various reasons to justify doing nothing when someone needs to be set free. The devil is the only one who has interest in an oppressed person not being set free.

Therefore we think that the Church should not be deprived of such an important ministry that is so needed by her members. Peter Horrobin said: "Conversion and deliverance were dealt with naturally, at one and the same time. I believe this was the normal practice of the early church and that one of the major reasons why deliverance ministry among Christians is often so hard is that the Church has not been ministering the New Testament pattern for salvation, healing and deliverance."[1]

The purpose of this book is to bring our modest contribution by making available a manual that will help to organize a ministry of deliverance in the local church and offer a guideline for the development of the deliverance minister. This manual will be used for instructional purposes in the local church to take deliverance ministry from a casual and informal activity, to an organized and established structure with every necessary component to function properly. This

---

[1] Peter Horrobin, *Healing Through Deliverance,* p.178.

manual will also provide the character requirements and the equipment and training necessary for the minister of deliverance to operate with excellence.

Three components are conceived, explained, and recommended for organizing the deliverance ministry and developing the deliverance minister: the teaching of deliverance, the anointing in the practice of deliverance, and the follow up of the deliverance.

Part 1
The Teaching Component of the Deliverance Ministry

The first component is teaching. Through this component people can acquire the knowledge of the cause of their struggle and gain an understanding of the process by which they can be set free. As a result, the ministry of deliverance can more easily get the willing participation of the people. Therefore, the teaching component of the deliverance ministry should involve two aspects: the biblical foundation of deliverance and a solid understanding of the deliverance process.

Chapter One

BIBLICAL FOUNDATION FOR DELIVERANCE

Deliverance Is a Covenant Right

Deliverance is, in Christ Jesus, a covenant right like sanctification, forgiveness of sins, and healing.

God Is the Author of Covenant Rights

In Genesis (6:18), God took the initiative to introduce to His creation the kind of agreement that He wanted between Him and them. He established a special agreement with man.

The English word for that agreement is *covenant*. The Hebrew root word translated by the noun covenant is *beriyth*, which also means confederacy. The corresponding verb is *karat* (to cut covenant). The New Testament Greek word is *diatheke*, which means contract or testament.

God, in covenant, takes the sole initiative. It is an initiative to establish a relationship of love and loyalty between

His people and Himself. God is interested in revealing to man His nature and character (love, goodness, faithfulness, etc.). For this purpose, God commits Himself to do some specific things for man in order to demonstrate to man His integrity in thought, word, and action. In the covenant, God involves Himself, His purpose, power, and provision. By this covenant, God is assuring man of His friendship and His choice to be on his side. Thus, God created a legal way for man to use the covenant and get God to act on his behalf. In fulfilling the covenant, God calls man to just respond to His love.

God Delivers Through Covenant

God intervened on behalf of the children of Israel because of His Covenant with Abraham. In the Book of Exodus, when the children of Israel were still in bondage in Egypt, the Bible says they cried and the Lord remembered His covenant with Abraham and He "had respect unto them." According to Exodus 2:23–25: "And it came to pass in process of time, that the king of Egypt died: and the children of Israel sighed by reason of the bondage, and they cried, and their cry came up unto God by reason of the bondage. And God heard their groaning, and God remembered His covenant with Abraham, with Isaac, and with Jacob. And God looked upon the children of Israel, and God had respect unto them."

The children of Israel, through prayer, had just activated the covenant that was theirs as heirs of Abraham. Deliverance is clearly a covenant right of the child of God and can be activated through prayer.

God Gives Priority to Covenant Right

The covenant right prevails over the observance of the Sabbath, as seen in the case of the woman in Luke 13:10–16.

Biblical Foundation for Deliverance

Jesus came into the synagogue and found this woman oppressed by a spirit of infirmity for eighteen years. Jesus was angry with the leaders of the synagogue, because this daughter of Abraham, He said, should not have suffered all these years but should have been delivered: "And ought not this woman, being a daughter of Abraham, whom Satan hath bound, lo, these eighteen years, be loosed from this bond on the Sabbath day?" But because of the hypocrisy of her leaders, she remained oppressed.

According to the Word of God, Christians are children of Abraham. Galatians 3:29 says: "And if ye be Christ's, then are ye Abraham's seed, and heirs according to the promise." Also, Galatians 4:7 says: "Wherefore thou art no more a servant, but a son; and if a son, then an heir of God through Christ." Therefore, as descendants of Abraham and sons of God by faith through Christ, not only do Christians have the same covenant rights, but they have even more than that, because, through the blood, the promises are even better (Hebrews 8:6).

It also appears that the law of love must prevail over the observance of the law of the Sabbath. It is important to mention that Jesus did not consider the rules of the synagogue, the Sabbath, the respect of the Sabbath, nor the observance of it, more valuable than expressing compassion to this woman by setting her free. The leaders of the synagogue, on the other hand, were more concerned in their hearts about the religious respect of the Sabbath than they felt need of this woman.

As a result, when Jesus saw the woman, His attitude was different from that of the leaders of the synagogue. He did not pass her by as did the priest in the parable of the Good Samaritan (Luke 10:30–37). He did not allow these things to stop Him from manifesting the love of God. Jesus, yielding to the love that rules His heart, was moved to deal with the situation of this woman. What an example of obedience to the two commandments in Matthew 22:37–40! So should the Church of the Lord Jesus Christ allow itself to be inspired and moved by the same love and attitude toward the oppressed?

As it appears here in the case of the woman, God gives a high priority to the release of His children through deliverance. This is so important to God that He is angered when it is neglected or when the infirmities of animals (in general, personal possessions) move the Church while the Church remains insensitive to the infirmities of His children (Luke 13:10–16).

God Uses Deliverance to Preserve and Maintain the Wellbeing of His Children

In the case of the Syrophenician woman in Mark 7:25, Jesus made it clear that she was not a part of the covenant because she was not a Jew. Therefore, she could not get her daughter freed from the oppression of the evil spirit; but because the woman was humble, prayed to the Lord, and refused to give up, Jesus was touched again with compassion and said, "Even though you don't have the right I will make an exception for you, go thy way because of your faith your daughter is free."

In this interaction with the Syrophenician woman, Jesus referred to deliverance as the children's bread. As bread is a staple food for the sustenance of our physical bodies, so deliverance maintains the spiritual wellbeing of the child of God. Therefore, according to Jesus, deliverance is a covenant right with an effect of maintaining the wellbeing of the child of God.

But the devil does not care about any rights. He will still try to prevent the covenanted child of God from enjoying his rights. That is why the child of God must know how

BIBLICAL FOUNDATION FOR DELIVERANCE

to exercise his authority if he will enjoy his rights; that is why in the process of deliverance people must be taught, trained, and taken to that point.

In conclusion, concerning covenant rights as a foundation of deliverance, it is established that God is a covenant-keeping God who works through His covenant to accomplish His will and manifest His love toward His children; and deliverance as part of God's covenant with His people is one of the most important expressions of that love and a means that God uses for His people's wellbeing.

Place and Role of Deliverance in the Christian's Spiritual Life

Place of Deliverance in the Christian's Spiritual Life

The second point that establishes a foundation for the deliverance ministry is the place of deliverance in the Christian life.

The need of deliverance after the new birth. In Obadiah 17, the Bible says: "But upon Mount Zion shall be deliverance, and there shall be holiness; and the house of Jacob shall possess their possessions."

A. First of all, what is Mount Zion?

- Mount Zion belongs to the Lord: "Yet have I set my King upon my holy hill of Zion" (Psalm 2:6).
- The Lord has founded Mount Zion: "What shall one then answer the messengers of the nations? That the Lord hath founded Zion, and the poor of his people shall trust in it" (Isaiah 14:32).
- The Lord has redeemed Mount Zion: "Remember thy congregation, which thou hast purchased of old, the

rod of thine inheritance, which thou hast redeemed, this Mount Zion wherein thou hast dwelt" (Psalm 74:2).
- Mount Zion has become the mountain of His holiness, the city of the great King: "Great is the Lord, and greatly to be praised in the city of our God, in the mountain of his holiness. Beautiful for situation, the joy of the whole earth, is mount Zion, on the sides of the north, the city of the great King" (Psalm 48:1–2).
- The Lord dwells in Mount Zion: "Sing praises to the Lord, which dwelleth in Zion; declare among the people his doings" (Psalm 9:11); "In Salem also is his tabernacle, and his dwelling place in Zion" (Psalm 76:2).

B. Today, Mount Zion is represented by the Christian. Today, Mount Zion, as the dwelling place of the Lord is not only a physical locality, but it is also represented by the Christians; those who are born again, those who have received in their spirit the Spirit of God and by the same fact carry the presence of God. That is considered Mount Zion in context of this reflection.

C. Deliverance is promised to Mount Zion: "But upon Mount Zion shall be deliverance…." (Obadiah 17). Deliverance is promised to Mount Zion, not just any kind of place but to the place where the Lord dwells. Deliverance is promised to the lives that carry the presence of God.

D. Mount Zion can be delivered. Mount Zion can be delivered because of the sure foundation, which is Jesus: "Therefore, thus saith the Lord God. Behold, I lay in Zion for a foundation a stone, a tried stone, a precious corner stone, a sure foundation...." Because that foundation is Jesus, righteousness is laid in the Christian heart; the refuge of lies and the hiding place of falsehood swept away. Because of the presence of Jesus in the heart of believers, every covenant with death against the Christians shall be disannulled, and the right of hell against them shall not stand (Isaiah 28:14–18).

Deliverance can be executed because of the presence of the Lord in one's life. As described in Obadiah, the chronology of transformation of the Christian life appears to include four steps in which deliverance comes after new birth and is followed by sanctification and prosperity.

Place of Deliverance in Sanctification

A. God's will for His people is their complete sanctification.

God, through Paul speaking to the Thessalonians, said: "For this is the will of God, even your sanctification, that ye should abstain from fornication" (1 Thessalonians 4:3). Paul went on to say precisely that God's will is a sanctification of the entire being: "And the very God of peace sanctify you wholly, and I pray God your whole spirit and soul and body be preserved blameless unto the coming of our Lord Jesus Christ."

(1 Thessalonians 5:23)

The promise of a new spirit has been made again and again, showing the insistence of God to get the sanctification of His people (Ezekiel 11:19, 18:31, 36:26; Romans 7:6). At new birth, the sanctification of the spirit occurs because we effectively receive a new spirit: "That which is born of the flesh is flesh; and that which is born of the Spirit is spirit" (John 3:6). After the new birth, God's will for the Christian is the sanctification of the rest of his being:

- In Christ, the Christian is created in righteousness and true holiness (Ephesians 4:24).
- His heart must be established in holiness (1 Thessalonians 3:13).
- He is a partaker of God's holiness (Hebrews 12:10).
- He must be yielding his "members as servants to righteousness unto holiness" (Romans 6:19).
- "Now the body is not for fornication, but for the Lord; and the Lord for the body" (1 Corinthians 6:13b).
- Christians are "bought with a price, therefore" they must "glorify God" in their "body and spirit, which are God's" (1 Corinthians 6:20).
- Christians "should know how to possess their vessel in sanctification and honor" (1 Thessalonians 4:4) "and holiness without which no man shall see the Lord" (Hebrews 12:14).
- The Christian's fruits should be "unto holiness, and the end everlasting life" (Romans 6:22), for he is not called "unto uncleanness but unto holiness" (1 Thessalonians 4:7).

For all this to happen, Christians must turn from the old way of thinking by thinking as God commanded in His Word: "I beseech you therefore, brethren, by the mercies of God, that ye present your bodies a living sacrifice, holy, acceptable unto God, which is your reasonable service. And be not conformed to this world; but be ye transformed by the renewing of your mind, that ye may prove what is that good, and acceptable, and perfect, will of God" (Romans 12:1–2).

    B. Deliverance is part of the necessary process needed to attain practical sanctification.
Practical sanctification is based on the new birth. It needs deliverance and renewing in order to develop. Without deliverance, the born-again person, already sanctified in terms of position in Christ, might have serious difficulties to live practically in sanctification. Can one stop practicing fornication while the spirit of fornication still operates in his life? As long as the spirit of lust is dominating one's emotional life and continues to produce unclean thoughts, one will be easily driven toward the physical act of fornication. After the sin is accomplished, people might suffer regret and sorrow because of the conviction of the Holy Spirit. But until power is exercised to cast out that spirit of lust, the condition probably will not change.

Those who might not be seriously sorrowful for their act and seem to "choose" to continue to disobey God by their unclean life of fornication constitute a special case that must first be brought to conviction and repentance before the unclean spirit is confronted.

But even for those who really do not want to fornicate, their condition will not change just because they do not want to fornicate. An actual dealing with the spirit being must take place in terms of casting it out of them.

C. Deliverance ushers sanctification in one's life.
Before confronting the overpowering evil spirit, there is a need of dealing with anything that benefits that spirit and can constitute his right in the lives of the oppressed persons: anything inside of them that allows the evil spirit to remain and continue keeping them oppressed and bound.

The fact is that people bear the responsibility for their oppression, because at some point they have, most of the time unknowingly, opened their lives to these spirits by choosing the pleasure of sin. "He that diggeth a pit shall fall into it; and whoso breaketh an hedge, a serpent shall bite him" (Ecclesiastes 10:8). Such people belong to one or both of these categories: the first category includes those who have opened their lives to evil spirits before the new birth. The second category includes those who were already born again before opening their lives to evil spirits. In both cases, they need a combined solution: the renewing of their mind by the Word of God coupled with the casting of the spirit beings out of their lives. In practice, this approach has allowed people to walk in sanctification who have been struggling in the church and sometimes discouraged even to the point of giving up. This act of getting rid of the evil entities from people's lives has its importance in practical sanctification. (Nevertheless, each instance of uncleanness in one's life is not created by demonic presence.)

Place of Sanctification in Prosperity

Finally, after the new birth, deliverance, and sanctification, comes prosperity: "the house of Jacob shall possess its possessions" (Obadiah 17). This is the place of prosperity, where people can receive their blessings. This place of blessing for God's people is subsequent to sanctification.

In 2 Corinthians 7:1, the Bible says: "Having therefore these promises, dearly beloved, let us cleanse ourselves from all filthiness of the flesh and spirit, perfecting holiness in the fear of God." Sanctification is given here as a condition for being properly positioned to get the benefit of the promises that God made to believers: believers must cleanse themselves from all filthiness including filthiness of the flesh and of spirit beings. Both filthiness of flesh and spirit prevent the believer from getting the blessings of God. In 2 Corinthians 6:14–18, just before He commanded sanctification, God made some fundamental promises to His people: "I will dwell in them, and walk in them; and I will be their God, and they shall be my people…I will receive you and will be a Father unto you, and you shall be my sons and daughters, saith the Lord Almighty." With these precious, vital, and exciting promises, God has put some clear conditions of sanctification that the child of God must always have in mind in order to daily practice them:

- Do not be yoked with unbelievers, no fellowship with unrighteousness, no communion with darkness;
- Have no concord with Belial, no part with infidels,
- Have no agreement with idols;
- Come out from among unrighteousness, darkness, Belial, infidels, idols, and be ye separate;
- Touch not the unclean thing.

Paul is speaking to born-again Christians: How can God warn about such things if they were not possible?

While dealing with entities and destroying their works through deliverance, and especially after getting a punctual breakthrough, the believer must infuse the Word of God into his system in order to attain and develop practical sanctification for his prosperity. And again, any result that is obtained through deliverance must be maintained and developed by getting the Word of God into the believer's system. Without this, there will not be a lasting prosperity in the Christian's life (3 John 2–4).

Role of Deliverance in the Christian's Spiritual Life: Facilitator of Fruitfulness

Importance of Christian fruitfulness:

    A. God expects fruitfulness.

        According to Genesis 1, God has repeatedly and clearly commanded the fruitfulness of His creation from the very beginning of its existence. Continually, throughout the Scriptures, from Genesis to Revelation, man specifically has been commanded by God to be fruitful. God has equipped him with His Word and His Spirit to make him fruitful. It is wisdom to consider any biblical means that could help especially the Christians become fruitful.

    B. Jesus reinforced the importance of fruitfulness.

        Jesus in many instances made fruitfulness the purpose for which He has chosen and sent His disciples. He promised that fruitfulness will cause our prayers to receive answers from the Father. Has He not said, "Ye have not chosen me, but I have chosen you, and ordained you, that ye should go and bring forth fruit, and that your fruit should remain: that whatsoever ye shall ask of the Father in my name, He may give it you" (John 15:16).

Jesus taught that fruitfulness is the proof that the believers—who are compared to branches—are properly connected to Him, the Vine. Jesus also established that fruitfulness is the way to glorify God and the criteria of truly being His disciple. In the same fifteenth chapter of the Book of John, Jesus said: "I am the Vine, ye are the branches: he that abides in me, and I in him, the same bringeth forth much fruit; for without me ye can do nothing…. If ye abide in me, and my words abide in you, ye shall ask what ye will, and it shall be done unto you. Herein is my Father glorified, that ye bear much fruit, so shall ye be my disciples" (John 15:5–8). And in Matthew, Jesus strongly warned His disciples about false prophets and recommended their fruits to be the criteria to discern them: "Ye shall know them by their fruits" (Matthew 7:16a).

Also, in the story of the fig tree to which Jesus came seeking for fruit, when He found nothing but leaves, Jesus showed no mercy to the unfruitfulness of the tree. He cursed the fig tree: "No man eats fruit of thee hereafter for ever" (Mark11:14). By so doing, Jesus was in fact putting emphasis in the conscience of His disciples on the seriousness of God's demand for fruitfulness and the dangerous consequences for unfruitfulness in a Christian's life. For the Bible said that Jesus made sure that His disciples heard Him cursing the fig tree (Mark 11:14b).

C. Fruitfulness distinguishes the Holy Spirit's presence and work.

The submission of one's life to the Holy Spirit and His work is characterized by the manifestation of the fruit of love, joy, peace, longsuffering, gentleness, goodness, faithfulness, meekness, and temperance (Galatians 5:22–24). No other spirit can manifest this fruit but the Spirit of God. The works of the flesh are conformed to the nature of Satan and his demons. They are as follows: adultery, fornication, uncleanness, lasciviousness, idolatry, witchcraft, hatred, variance, emulations, wrath, strife, seditions, heresies, envying, murders, drunkenness, reveling, and such like (Galatians 5:19–21).

These works grieve the Spirit of God and attract evil spirits who attach themselves to an individual in order to oppress the person. It is therefore obvious that the fruit of the Spirit is a sign of God's manifested presence and preventive equipment of effective protection against every demonic attack and oppression.

Deliverance and the Fruit of Glorifying God

God instructed His people to give thanks, pay their vows to Him, and pray to Him so that He would deliver them and they would glorify Him (Psalm 50:14–15).

God also commanded His people to get rid of anything that is not of the light from their lives (Ephesians 5:11), expel demons and destroy their works, and break hindrances to their transformation by the Word and the Spirit. He wants the light of Christ to shine brighter through His people so men may see their good works and glorify Him (Matthew 5:16).

Christians must therefore be careful to not ignorantly reject any means given by God to deal with conditions that may determine their fruitfulness.

BIBLICAL FOUNDATION FOR DELIVERANCE

Jesus' Strategy for Fruitfulness

In Mark 4:3–19, teaching His disciples about fruitfulness in the kingdom of God, Jesus compared the Christian life to the ground where a sower would sow a seed. He also warned His disciples concerning the importance of this parable of the sower for the understanding of all parables. That is to say that understanding is a major key for the work of the kingdom of God. He specifically defined four categories of ground:

A. The first category of ground:

> "And these are they by the way side, where the word is sown; but when they have heard, Satan cometh immediately, and take away the word that was sown in their hearts."
>
> (Mark 4:15)

This category refers to people who hear the Word: the Word is sown in their hearts. But Jesus indicates that the fowls of the air come immediately and devour the seed: Satan comes immediately and takes it away.

Thus, Jesus qualified the problem of getting the Word of God into the Christian's life as being first a spiritual problem. The misunderstanding or the neglect of the demonic root as being the first cause of the problem of growth and maturity in a Christian's life is mainly responsible for the ineffectiveness of the strategies deployed to cause the development of people in the church.

First things must be taken care of first. Dealing with Satan and his demons must be at the core of any strategy designed to solve the problem of sowing the Word of God for fruitfulness. The Word of God is precious. It is worthy of considering for ways to get it effectively into the ground without being hindered. One of the reasons why Jesus gave this parable to His disciples is because He wanted them to be so mindful of the hindrances they would have to deal with. Jesus wants the sower to be a true sower not one who scatters—teaching and preaching God-given messages—without being concerned about the receptivity of the recipient.

There was a former Muslim man who used to come to our church years ago. While he was being prayed for after the new birth, a demon said that he was in his ears to prevent him from hearing the Word. Because of this kind of demon, a person can keep coming to church as did this brother without experiencing any significant spiritual growth. But by the grace of God this former Muslim man was delivered from that demon, and today he is serving the Lord as a missionary pastor in a Muslim country.

B. The second category of ground:

In the case of the second category of ground, it refers to the seed coming upon it, but it cannot take root because of the stony nature of the ground. There is not much earth for the seed. Immediately when the sun is up the seed is scorched, and because it has no root, it withers away. Jesus explained that these people, when they heard the Word, immediately receive it with gladness but have no root in themselves and so endure but for a time. These people are superficial. They do not take time to meditate upon the Word; neither do they deal with some character issues in their lives such as weak commitment to the things of God, bitterness, or general bad attitudes. Jesus said that when affliction or persecution arises for the Word's sake, immediately these people are offended. They question God's character and have no trust in Him. Since there is no root in them, there is no understanding to make them see their way through.

Here, Jesus describes natural causes as predominant. Therefore, the issue must be dealt with as being primarily a simple problem of understanding. In the case of a non-satisfactory solution, it is not anti-scriptural to consider the hypothesis of a demonic involvement and to confront the demon. A demonic spirit can obviously influence the understanding in terms of bringing confusion of the mind or emotional distraction.

C. The third category of ground:

The third category of ground is the one where the seed is sown among thorns. Jesus explained that the Word is heard, but the cares of this world, the deceitfulness of riches, and the lusts of other things enter in, choke the Word, and it becomes unfruitful. These kinds of people are not yet following after things like righteousness, godliness, faith, love, patience, and meekness. In fact, they are open to foolish and hurtful lusts. These doors, because of worldliness, will ultimately work in favor of demonic spirits.

To keep this category of person from falling into such destructive temptations and snares of perdition, it will take a treatment involving dealing with spiritual forces and destroying their works. Or else, what profit is there to continue sowing seeds (of the Word) that are choked unto unfruitfulness? If the very Word that is supposed to destroy strongholds becomes unfruitful, it is a clear indication that the causes of this unfruitfulness must first be dealt with in order to get an environment where the Word can be fruitful. For nothing is wrong with the seed. But here, the fruitfulness is not determined only by the quality of the seed but also by the state of the environment in which it is sown.

D. The fourth category of ground:

The last category of ground is the good one. This is the only ground where the seed can produce fruits. Even in this context, Jesus made it clear that there are many levels of fruitfulness: a 30 percent level, a 60 percent level, and a 100 percent level.

There are still some questions: why should someone stay at a 30 percent level of fruitfulness while he could develop up to the 60 percent level? It only takes a certain treatment of the ground to make such a qualitative transformation. Also, why should one stay at a 60 percent level of fruitfulness while he could develop up to the 100 percent level? It only takes another kind of treatment of the ground to make such a qualitative transformation. The ground needs to be prepared until the fruitfulness reaches the 100 percent level. Jesus is saying that there must always be a preparation of the ground. Also, the sower might be limited in terms of knowing the ground in which he is sowing.

These considerations indicate that there must be a systematic approach to preparing the ground: there is the need of a support system to the ministration of the Word. That support can be properly called a ministry of deliverance whose function is to prepare the ground for the ministry of the Word.

So, the first part is the preparation in the Word of God. The sower must prepare himself in terms of studying, praying, fasting, and putting in the effort and hours needed to receive God's message. This is absolutely necessary. But, if there is no preparation of the ground to receive God's message, most of the efforts of the sower will be limited. Therefore, the deliverance ministry should back up the efforts of the ministration of the Word by taking care of the ground, making people understand and fight for their rights to be good ground, helping them to prepare the ground by removing all roots of unfruitfulness: Satan and demonic spirits, superficiality, offense, cares of this world, deceitfulness of riches, lusts, and anything that could choke the Word and make it unfruitful. For instance, the minister could pray for people: "Lord, let there be a good ground in your people to receive the Word" and also deal with demonic spirits in order to cast them out and destroy their works.

In conclusion, it is obvious that Jesus' strategy for fruitfulness includes the preparation of the ground for the seed. Also, Jesus is warning that the sower will reap according to what he has sown but also according to how he has prepared the ground in which he has sown. And this is where deliverance is involved.

The Role of the Church in Deliverance

The Church must help believers to be aware of the danger posed both by the flesh and by demons. Satan and his demons have their most astonishing success in leading many Christians into gross error of doctrine and conduct through false teaching and teachers. "To deny the possibility of the demonic working in the lives of Christians is to fail to allow Scripture to speak in the full scope of its implications and to flatly ignore experience. To fail to grasp the full extent to which such sinister power may operate is perilous, for it denies to those who have been invaded by the enemy the understanding and help they so desperately need. Also, this teaching warns those uninvaded of the peril of invasion and of what will happen if they fail to reckon on what they are in Christ and backslide into gross and willful sin."[3]

The Bible warns the Church about false teachings and doctrines of demons: "Now the Spirit speaketh expressly, that in the latter times some shall depart from the faith, giving heed to seducing spirits, and doctrines of devils" (1 John 4:1).

The early Church held to the reality of demons and demonization. There is no spectacle more tragic than to see a Christian spoiled doctrinally by Satan, blinded by error, and bound under the delusion and enslavement of demonic teaching. What must the Church do in the light of all this evidence?

The Church must be willing to obey the Great Commission (Matthew 28:18–20). According to the Great Commission, the Church must obey all things that the Lord Jesus commanded, even before teaching others to obey them. Among the things commanded by the Lord, deliverance

---
[3] Merrill E. Unger in *What Demons Can Do to Saints*, page 94.

is repeatedly mentioned. From the very beginning of their ministry, to His departure from them, the Lord gave His disciples authority and commanded them to oppose unclean spirits in order to cast them out from where they are. In Matthew 10:1, 7, when the disciples were only twelve in number, the Lord commanded them to go and do the work of the kingdom and cast out unclean spirits. Again, when the number of disciples increased to seventy, the Lord did not change that command. He sent them in Luke 9:1–2 to go and do the work of the kingdom and cast out unclean spirits; for, when they returned to Him (Luke 10:17), they reported that even the evil spirits were subject to them in His name. Before departing from His disciples, the Lord again reminded them of the same command saying, "These signs shall follow them that believe: In my name they shall cast out demons...." (Mark 16:17). Jesus not only commanded deliverance, He also made deliverance one of the purposes for which He came (Luke 4:18). He even went further by actually demonstrating deliverance all over the place wherever He went. Note that, most of the time, wherever He went, deliverance was possible because of His presence and His authority (see Matthew 12:22–30; Mark 5:1–20, 9:14–29; Luke 4:33–36, 40–41, 13:10–17).

In the instance where Pharisees came to warn the Lord of King Herod's intentions to arrest Him for His activities and kill Him, the Lord made it clear that He would not stop casting out demons: "Go ye, and tell that fox, behold, I cast out devils, and I do cures today and tomorrow, and the third day I shall be perfected." And He has not changed His mind from casting out demons, for even after He died and rose from the grave, He still commanded His disciples to go and cast demons out (Mark 16:17–20; Matthew 28:18–20).

As His body, the Church must seek to do what the Head did. In fact, the Lord is still doing deliverance, through those who allow themselves to be His hands, mouth, and feet today, as part of His work of establishing His kingdom (Matthew 12:28).

The Church must believe and stand on the finished works of Jesus (Hebrews 9:13–14). In order to execute deliverance, the Church must believe and arise on the basis of the finished works of Jesus at the cross of Calvary.

- Jesus destroyed the old man. At the cross, Jesus destroyed the old man and the body of sin: "Knowing this, that our old man is crucified with Him, that the body of sin might be destroyed, that henceforth we should not serve sin" (Romans 6:6).
- Jesus destroyed the devil. At the cross, Jesus destroyed the devil: "Forasmuch as the children are partakers of flesh and blood, he also Himself likewise took part of the same; that through death He might destroy Him that had the power of death, that is, the devil" (Hebrews 2:14). In reality, what Jesus did at the cross has affected the devil in an irreversible way that is equivalent to destruction without possibility of recovery. That is more than a simple defeat with the possibility of recovery and revenge. That reminds us of the words of Maschil of Asaph: "For God is my King of old, working salvation in the midst of the earth. Thou didst divide the sea by thy strength: thou brakest the heads of the dragons in the waters. Thou brakest the heads of leviathan in pieces, and gavest him to be meat to the people inhabiting the wilderness" (Psalm 74:12–14). Moreover, Jesus took back the power of death from the hand of Satan as far as Christians are concerned. The Bible said clearly that He destroyed he who had the power of death. He also took back the key of Hades.

- Jesus freed us and brought us under the law of the Spirit of life. At the cross, Jesus has freed us from the law of sin and death: "There is therefore now no condemnation to them which are in Christ Jesus, who walk not after the flesh, but after the Spirit. For the law of the Spirit of life in Christ Jesus hath made me free from the law of sin and death" (Romans 8:1–2). The law under which we now live and depart from the earth is another law, which is the law of the Spirit of life in Christ Jesus. No condemnation can work under the law of the Spirit of life in Christ Jesus. The spirit of death entered human life as a condemnation because of the fall of man in sin. Now, in Christ Jesus, under the law of the Spirit of life, the Spirit of life is the One in charge of our life (on earth) and our departure (to heaven). We move out of here by the Spirit of life. Just as we remove our physical clothes. The spirit of death (Revelation 6:8) can never overpower the one who is under the control of the Spirit of life, who walks not after the flesh but after the Spirit.
- Jesus destroyed the authority of the satanic armed forces. At the cross, Jesus has disarmed all satanic principalities and powers and exposed them to public shame (Colossians 2:15).
- Jesus destroyed the works of darkness. Jesus has destroyed all evil works by His blood: "He that committeth sin is of the devil, for the devil sinneth from the beginning. For this purpose the son of God was manifested, that He might destroy the works of the devil" (1 John 3:8).
- Jesus sanctified us by His blood. At the cross, Jesus purged us from all dead works by His blood: "how much more shall the blood of Christ, who through

the eternal Spirit offered Himself without spot to God, purge your conscience from dead works to serve the living God?" (Hebrews 9:14). Again: "For by one offering He hath perfected for ever them that are sanctified" (Hebrews 10:14), and "from Jesus Christ, who is the faithful witness, and the first begotten of the dead, and the prince of the kings of the earth. Unto Him that loved us, and washed us from our sins in His own blood, and hath made us kings and priests unto God and His Father; to Him be glory and dominion for ever and ever. Amen" (Revelation 1:5–6).

The Church must have compassion to visit and pray for the oppressed. In Ezekiel 16:1–9, God said: "Again the word of the Lord came unto me, saying, Son of man, cause Jerusalem to know her abominations, and say, thus saith the Lord God unto Jerusalem; thy birth and thy nativity is of the land of Canaan; thy father was an Amorite, and thy mother an Hittite. And as for thy nativity, in the day thou wast born thy navel was not cut, neither wast thou washed in water to supple thee;...none eye pitied thee, to do any of these unto thee, to have compassion upon thee; but thou wast cast out in the open field, to the loathing of thy person, in the day that wast born."

There is an inspiring situation concerning deliverance and what the Church should be doing. The Spirit of God was speaking through the prophet and said: "Tell Jerusalem that I hold these abominations against her." And the Spirit of God addresses Jerusalem as if Jerusalem was a human being, saying:

BIBLICAL FOUNDATION FOR DELIVERANCE

- Abomination due to birth and nativity circumstances: "Your birth and your nativity are of the land of Canaan."
  God called abomination the land where the birth of Jerusalem took place. This certainly is referring to the idolatry practiced in the land by the Canaanites. Remember that the first instruction God gave to the children of Israel as He sent them to possess the land of Canaan was to prevent them from falling into idolatry: "Take heed to thyself, lest thou make a covenant with the inhabitants of the land whither thou goest, lest it be for a snare in the midst of thee. But ye shall destroy their altars, break their images, and cut down their groves: for thou shalt worship no other god, for the Lord, whose name is Jealous is a jealous God" (Exodus 34:12–14). These practices in the land of the birth of Jerusalem have been called the abominations of Jerusalem.
- Abomination due to ancestors: "Your father was an Amorite and your mother an Hittite." Another abomination for Jerusalem is due to its familial background.
- Abomination due to the navel: "as for thy nativity, in the day that thou wast born thy navel was not cut." The Spirit, through Ezekiel, continued saying that another abomination is due to the navel by which the iniquities of past generations were transferred to Jerusalem. Note that there is no physical navel for a city. God is talking about a spiritual navel. Therefore, we human beings, having a physical navel at birth should be even more careful to deal with the spiritual one.
- God is concerned about indifference to deliverance: "None eye pitied thee, to do any of these unto thee,

to have compassion upon thee; but thou wast cast out in the open field, to the loathing of thy person, in the day that thou wast born" (Ezekiel 16:5).

God was apparently grieved because He expected that someone would have compassion on Jerusalem to deal with each one of these realities in Jerusalem's life, for in His eyes these are abominations. Therefore God has to send His prophet to point out such lack of compassion.

These aspects of Jerusalem's life have their correspondences in the life of God's people today and the need to deal with them is also real today. The Church cannot leave people to themselves regarding these abominations after the new birth. People cannot be abandoned and left to their own devices. God said that such an attitude reflects a lack of compassion. Compassion should cause the Church to do the treatment required for the people to be freed from what God called abominations.

When Jesus came to Earth, He exercised that compassion. The Church ought to have Christ's compassion. This compassion is crucial if anyone will minister deliverance.

The Church must exercise authority and power against evil. Before giving the Great Commission, Jesus determined the context in which He wanted the Church to work it out. He said in Matthew 28:18 that "all authority is given unto me in heaven and in earth. Go ye therefore..."

In Matthew 10:1, when He first called His disciples, the only equipment He gave them was authority (*exousia*). Charles H. Kraft said that: "Since we are created in the image and the likeness of God (Genesis 1:26), we are higher by creation in both position and authority than even Satan and his angels. We are God's masterpiece, created high above every other creature, including the angels."[4] The proper relationship with God, through the works of Christ appropriated by faith, means the restoration of the authority lost through Adam.

All the signs in Mark 16:17–18 were to be the result of the Church exercising the authority of the name of Jesus. In Mark 9:14–29, Jesus was disappointed at His disciples when they failed to exercise authority in order to get the child freed from demonic oppression. He did not say that they had small faith. He called them a "faithless generation."

These were people who had left everything to follow Him; they were with Him on a daily basis; they saw and believed Him when He performed miracles. But Jesus, in this instance, said: "I don't count your faith as faith if you cannot do this; how long shall I be with you? You are supposed to be doing this." So, Jesus greatly expected that His disciples would be able to deal with this situation; that is why He considered that their faith was not strong enough. They needed to commune more with Him in His Word spoken to them, in prayer and also in fasting.

The Church must exercise the authority of the Word of God spoken in the authority of the name of Jesus in order to enjoy the benefits of her covenant with God, including deliverance.

The Church must equip the believers to stand and resist. Believers must absolutely be taught and trained to pray to God and to resist in spiritual warfare (James 4:7). These two arts represent one of the weakest aspects of a lot of Christians today. As a result, many cannot really

---

[4] Charles H. Kraft, *I Give You Authority,* p.136.

exercise their faith and become abnormally dependent upon others.

The Church must establish and develop the ministry of deliverance. In Luke 4:33–38 and 13:10–16, Jesus did not just recognize the right of the man and the woman to be delivered; He actually took the steps to deliver them. There is a need of not only recognizing the covenant right of believers to be freed, but there is even a far greater need to set structures in the Church that will systematically deliver those who come to the synagogue (the Church) bound.

It happened one time that the Church failed to do it, and you see how Jesus called them faithless in the Book of Mark (Mark 9:19)! In Matthew 10:1 and Luke 9:1–2, He gave them authority to oppose unclean spirits and that opposition should end up by casting out demons. In the Book of Mark (Mark 16:17), He said these are the signs that should follow them that believe in Him: they should cast out demons.

Questionnaire

1. What was established between God and man in Genesis 6:18?

   _____

   _____

2. On which basis did God intervene on behalf of the children of Israel?

   _____

   _____

Biblical Foundation for Deliverance

3. How could the children of Israel have activated their covenant right? And could you activate your covenant right?

   _____

   _____

4. What makes our covenant of greater priority, as compared to the observance of the Sabbath?

   _____

   _____

5. What attitude does God expect us to observe as a principle toward people and specifically as related to their right to be delivered?

   _____

   _____

6. Do we need deliverance after the new birth?

   _____

   _____

7. Is deliverance involved in attaining the whole sanctification?

   _____

   _____

8. How did Jesus reinforce the importance of fruitfulness?

   _____

   _____

9. What role must the Church play in order to help Christian spiritual growth?

   _____

   _____

10. What means are available to the Church to operate deliverance?

    _____

    _____

11. What actions should the Church take to get the believers alert and prepared to fight?

    _____

    _____

Chapter Two

UNDERSTANDING DELIVERANCE

Definition of Deliverance

Explanation of the Hebrew/Greek Root Term[5]

    A. The Hebrew/Greek words translated by the English verb *deliver* cover various meanings. Some words are rendered as "deliver" in English, but they mean rather "to give over," "to surrender," "to come forth, appear, and exist as by birth." These words have been excluded. Here are the only words that fit in the context of this study: the Hebrew word *natsal* is the most used in the Old Testament. The *natsal* meanings are: to snatch away (good or bad sense), defend, deliver (self), preserve, escape, recover, rescue, save, spoil, strip, take (out).

    The Hebrew words translated *salvation: yzhuah* (aid); *tzhuah* (rescue: literally or figuratively, personal,

---

[5] See attached, the other Hebrew/Greek terms translated by *deliverance*.

national or spiritual); *yesha* (liberty, prosperity); *mozhaah* (deliverance). The Greek word translated *salvation*: *soteria* (only word for salvation in the New Testament, used forty-three times: rescue or safety [physically or morally]: deliver, health, save, saving).

B. The terminologies "salvation" and "deliverance": As regarding these root meanings, the terms deliverance and salvation appear to be, to a certain extent, interchangeable. It can be interpreted by the fact that at salvation deliverance begins. It might continue and produce fruits depending on the effectiveness of one's Christian life.

At the point of the new birth, the coming in of the Holy Spirit drives out many evil spirits, especially those that were dwelling in the area of one's spirit. That is common to all those who accept Jesus as their personal Lord and Savior. In the areas of the soul, the body, the relationship, and the possessions, it is obvious in the Scriptures that some transformation is still needed.

Deliverance Is a Continual Process

The process of deliverance is in fact a continual one. It takes place in three different times. In the Book of 2 Corinthians, it is stated: "who delivered us from so great death, and doth deliver; in whom we trust that he will yet deliver us" (2 Corinthians 1:10).

God Has Already Delivered Us

"Delivered us from so great death" refers to freedom from the possession of the power of darkness and translation into the kingdom of God (Colossians 1:13).

UNDERSTANDING DELIVERANCE

God Is Delivering Us Now

"And doth deliver" refers to sanctification of the soul, body, and all related things. This sanctification includes the renewing of the mind. It is both a part and a prolongation of the release from the oppression of the powers of darkness and the works that they introduced into the lives of God's people before they got saved: "For this purpose, the Son of God was manifested, that He might destroy the works of the devil" (1 John 3:8). This was fulfilled at the cross of Calvary. God's people can appropriate what Jesus did by believing in Him and acting upon His words: "If ye continue in my word (after believing in me) then are ye my disciples indeed; and ye shall know the truth, and the truth shall make you free" (John 8:31–32). Deliverance here means dislodging the demonic spirit from any part of God's people and destroying their curses, sicknesses, etc. Demons must be cast out and their works destroyed by commands that release the power of the Holy Spirit. Renewing of the mind is a process that takes time in the Word of God and the help of the Holy Spirit. It involves a conscious and continual effort by God's people while deliverance is relatively an act of God that only requires willingness and practical cooperation.

In both cases, each Christian has the responsibility of cooperating with the Holy Spirit to get this present deliverance work in his life for effective renewing of the mind and sanctification: "for if ye live after the flesh, ye shall die: but if ye through the spirit do mortify the deeds of the body, ye shall live" (Romans 8:13).

God Will Deliver Us

"In whom we trust that He will yet deliver us" refers to making a way of escape in every temptation. God's faithfulness is manifested in that He watches over His people. God does not allow His people to be taken captive just because the enemy tempts them: "but God is faithful, who will not suffer you to be tempted above that ye are able; but will with the temptation also make a way to escape, that ye may be able to bear it" (1 Corinthians 10:13). God is faithful to make His people escape, and also God knows how to do it: "The Lord knoweth how to deliver the godly out of temptations…." (2 Peter 2:9). Remember that Jesus taught His disciples to pray for this deliverance: "And lead us not into temptation, but deliver us from evil…." (Matthew 6:13a).

Deliverance involves:

- being smashed from the power of darkness (getting out of Egypt),
- being released by getting spirits expelled out and cleansed from their works (getting Egypt out of God's people),
- being freed from evil snares by receiving a way of escape.

Purpose of Deliverance

From the Fall to Redemption

Before the fall, man had been walking with God. Man had communion with God. Because of sin, man was afraid of that which he used to have fellowship with: "And they heard the voice of the Lord God walking in the garden in the cool of the day. And Adam and his wife hid themselves from the presence of the Lord God amongst the trees of the garden" (Genesis 3:8). From the fall up to the redemption, man remained excluded from the fellowship with God. It is only when Jesus went to the cross, shed His blood, and redeemed man from sin and its consequences that man was once again able to have a relationship with God.

The instant transformation of the spirit of man. Redemption brought a complete transformation of mankind: "Therefore if any man be in Christ, he is a new creature: old things are passed away; behold, all things are become new" (2 Corinthians 5:17). Such a man is a new creature in Christ Jesus because the spirit man is automatically transformed. It is a new spirit, one that is able to commune with God again. The spirit is born again and regenerated. The dominator, who is Satan, no longer has authority over the spirit man who is owned by the Lord Jesus Christ and exclusively indwelled by the Holy Spirit. It is important to note here that the transformation of the spirit man occurs instantly. As soon as a person accepts the Lord Jesus, the spirit man is completely and instantly regenerated. But it is not so for the soul (will, mind, emotions) and the body.

The progressive transformation of the areas of the soul and the body. In fact, the Bible begs the Christian to "renew" his mind. What need is there to renew something if it has already been renewed through the new birth? That leads us to believe that some old things still reside in the soul and must be addressed. For the transformation to take place, the Holy Spirit requires of the believer a conscious and diligent participation. This is where each one must take the responsibility to allow the Holy Spirit to work at the transformation by giving himself to a regular meditation of the Word of God. There is no other way to change the old way of thinking except by the Word of God. Such transformation does not occur instantly. It is a process that must be developed in time.

Then, a progressive transformation will take place as opposed to the instant regeneration of the spirit of man. The same process must be developed for the emotions as believers are commanded to "set (their) affection on things above, not on things on the earth" (Colossians 3:2). The will, which is a part of the soul, must also be progressively transformed by the same process in order to be conformed to the will of God.

In the case of the body, even the body of a born-again Christian, it can still suffer sicknesses and diseases. That is not God's will for him. God's will is for him to be healed and to stay in good health beyond just receiving healing (3 John 2). God's will for the newborn Christian is that he might prosper and be in good health, meaning that he should be in good health every day of his life.

Again, it is one's responsibility to give himself to the meditation of the Word of God so to allow the Holy Spirit to work in him. Such a transformation will require time and continual effort in the Word and in obedience.

Therefore, the born-again Christians, after having their spirits instantly regenerated, also have the privilege and the means to get their soul renewed and their body in good health. In the three dimensions of the human being, effectively they are new creatures. It was not so before the new-birth experience. The old things are passed away.

Nevertheless, some old things that have been brought from the former sinful life remain active in the new creature and must be dealt with. It is important to know that these old things are the elements that Satan, former dominator, can use to try to get one back to him. In these attempts, he uses demons to accomplish his goals. These demons might find their way into the soul and the body where the Holy Spirit is not dwelling.

Thus, they can easily and legally oppress the soul and the body that are to be transformed.

It is now obvious that the soul and the body can be the siege of a war between the Holy Spirit and the demons. The Christians are the ones who must choose to disallow demons to work in them and to allow the Holy Spirit to help them by reckoning themselves "to be indeed dead unto sin but alive unto God" (Romans 6:11). They are the ones who should choose. It is a personal choice as much as salvation itself is. That choice means that one must develop himself in the truth of God's Word:

> Knowing this, that our old man is crucified with Him (Christ), that the body of sin might be destroyed, that henceforth we should not serve sin.
> (Romans 6:6)

> I am crucified with Christ; nevertheless I live, yet not I, but Christ liveth in me; and the life which I now live in the flesh I live by the faith of the Son of God, who loved me, and gave himself for me.
> (Galatians 2:20)

> And they that are Christ's have crucified the flesh with the affections and lusts.
> (Galatians 5:24)

> But God forbid that I should glory, save in the cross of our Lord Jesus Christ, by whom the world is crucified unto me, and I unto the world.
> (Galatians 6:14)

While developing in the truth, one must also fight the demonic spirits that try to take advantage of things to conform people to their nature that they might oppress one.

Besides this inner private fight, there is another fight that is external, personal, and collective: "For we wrestle not against flesh and blood, but against principalities, against powers, against the rulers of the darkness of this world, against spiritual wickedness in high places" (Ephesians 6:12).

In order to successfully take part in this war, all new believers—Christians—must "be strong in the Lord, and in the power of His might (and) put on the whole armor of God that (they) may be able to stand against the wiles of the devil" (Ephesians 6:10–11).

Now, the spiritual reality of the born-again Christian is comparable to the physical reality of a newborn, which is helpless, weak, dependent, unequipped, and inexperienced. That is why those Christians who are mature must take upon themselves, as natural parents do for their babies, the responsibilities to help develop the newly born-again Christians. No matter how much these mature Christians are helping the newborn ones, they will have very little success in making them advance without removing the ties and bondages that keep them immobile. In order to deal with the root (cause) instead of the branches, they should drive out any evil spirit responsible for the bondages. That is the purpose of deliverance ministry. The ideal situation is that every person be able to meditate in the Word of God, obey the Word of God, believe the Word of God, and confess and stand upon the Word in his/her circumstances. The life of such a person will probably become a self-processed deliverance, if he knows how to prepare himself in terms of deliverance.

Unfortunately, the ideal case is an exception. Not all people who just come to the Lord are at the level where they can pray for themselves. Most of the people who come need to be taken by the hand like spiritual babies. They need to be taught how to prepare themselves in terms of deliverance, how to stand to fight and be free. Some don't even confess the Word; when they are told that the Word has to become abundant in their heart, they don't understand: how will it work for them?

UNDERSTANDING DELIVERANCE

Following is the drawing of the story of man from the fall to the redemption:

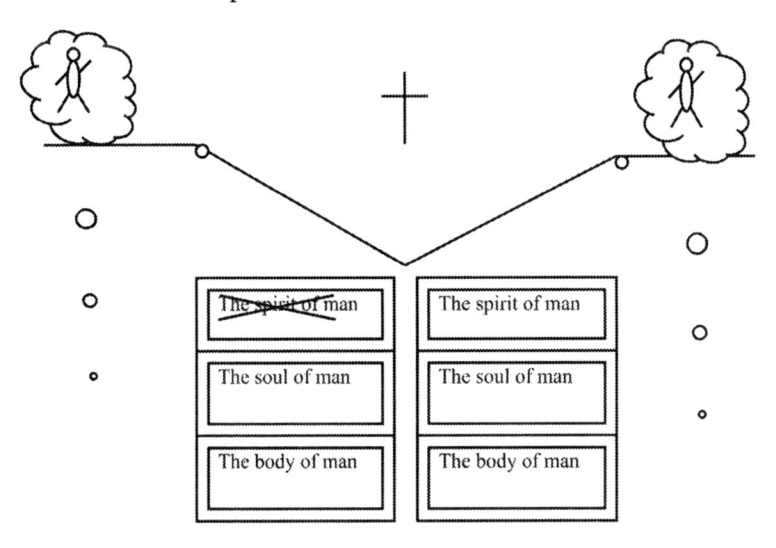

1. Man was in the presence of God (Genesis 1:26). God created man in His own image in order to have communion with Him. That is why man was able to hear and to converse with God. Man was aware of God's presence and was in harmony with Him until sin came in and the fellowship was broken.
2. Man is separated from the presence of God (Romans 3:23, 10). Under the temptation of Satan, man sinned. Sin began to reign in human life. The spirit of man was no longer able to commune with God. Man lost his ability to hear God and to be sensitive to His presence. In fact, the spirit of man died as far as his original purpose was concerned. The soul became exposed to evil thoughts, ungodly affections, and rebellion in the will. Sickness and diseases could therefore affect the body and bring destruction. Death entered human life

(Romans 6:23a). Henceforth, man became an object of Satan's obsession, oppression, and even possession.

3. Man became a new creation in Christ. The love and the grace of God expressed through the sacrifice of Jesus at the cross of Calvary redeemed man back to his fellowship with God. The crucifixion, the death, and the resurrection have given to man victory over sin, Satan, death, and hell. Man became a new creation in Christ. Jesus is his Lord and his legal Owner. The works of Christ have brought a complete transformation of the entire being of man. Although complete transformation may not yet be manifested, man is no more the object of Satan's dominion. Satan has no more right to keep man under the former status, but he would not abandon by himself his grips over man. It takes confrontation and power to expel him from man's life. That is where spiritual warfare and deliverance enter in.

4. Man is restored back to the presence of God. The renewed spirit of man is now sensitive to God's presence and can commune with Him. Man can now receive instructions, directions, and guidance from God. Man can thus interact properly. Man and God can agree and walk together once again. Man becomes therefore a co-laborer with God. This restoration will take place according to man's obedience regarding his responsibility in terms of renewing the mind by the Word of God, setting his affections where Christ is sitting, submitting his will to the will of God, and holding his members (his body) in righteousness.

The Temple of the Holy Ghost

It is important to know that before the shed blood of Jesus, the temple was composed of the outer court, the inner court, and the holy place where all the ceremonies were done. Jesus, when He came in the outer court and saw the merchants, cast them out (John 2:13–15). That was before the shedding of His blood for our sin. Today, Christians are the temple of God (1 Corinthians 3:16, 6:19).

As in the temple of God today, Jesus is still making sure that anything preventing the free worship in His temple is cast out. Those evil spirits, like the merchants in the temple in Jesus' time, need also to be cast out. So we are called to be coworkers with Christ by helping Him to cast out these spirits from people's lives and by destroying their works, in order for true worship to take place. Most of the time, when someone finishes his/her deliverance, he/she feels like praising God. One of the results of deliverance is that people will move into loving and worshiping the Lord quite spontaneously and with involvement of their hearts. We have to pull out the weapons and then command the spirits to leave. Once these things are out, the real praise and real worship will come.

Making Room for the Holy Ghost in Other Areas

There is a need to help people make enough room for the Holy Ghost. As long as evil spirits have ground, rights, and do their works, the Holy Ghost is limited. The Holy Ghost will not force Himself on anyone. He will do what one allows Him. He respects the will of the person, but a demon will force his way in. So we should tell the new believers that they need to repent, renounce the evil grounds and doors. This will allow the Holy Spirit to work and deliver.

Types of people who benefit from deliverance:

- Unbeliever delivered

  Mark 5:1–20 gives the account of the Gadarene man, probably an unbeliever who was really delivered, because right after Jesus had cast out the spirits from him, he had a strong desire to follow Jesus. He even witnessed to others in Decapolis. The mercy of God is unlimited.

- Believers being delivered

  In the Book of Mark, Jesus cast out a demonic spirit from a man in the synagogue: "And there was in their synagogue a man with an unclean spirit; and he cried out…And Jesus rebuked him, saying, hold thy peace, and come out of him. And when the unclean spirit had torn him, and cried with a loud voice, he came out of him" (Mark 1:23–27). This scenario is repeated in Luke 13:10–16 with the woman who had a spirit of infirmity: "And he was teaching in one of the synagogues on the sabbath. And, behold, there was a woman which had a spirit of infirmity eighteen years, and was bowed together, and could in no wise lift up herself…."

  Were these believers? The context of the synagogue chosen by the Spirit of God and especially the covenant mentioned in the case of the woman lead to the conclusion that these were believers who had been delivered.

- Case showing a default of deliverance

  In the Book of Acts, Simon's case indicated that a believer must be willing to renounce any form of idolatry in order to be really delivered. Simon was a sorcerer who believed, burned his equipments of practicing witchcraft, and became Simon the former sorcerer: "Then Simon himself believed also: and when he was baptized, he continued with Philip, and wondered, beholding the miracles and signs which were done" (Acts 8:13). Nevertheless, Simon still had the spirit of witchcraft and needed to be delivered of it. Peter ended up rebuking Simon who finally expressed a prayer request that should have led to a deliverance session. This situation happens frequently in the Church. Most of the time, those who need deliverance prayer do not receive proper assistance.

- Cases for future deliverance

The Book of Corinthians (2 Corinthians 11:4) refers to the possibility for believers to receive a spirit (which, by implication, has not yet been received): meaning that believers can still receive another spirit, a spirit who is different from the Holy Spirit they already received: "For if he that cometh preacheth another Jesus, whom we have not preached, or if ye receive another spirit, which ye have not received, or another gospel, which ye have not accepted, ye might well bear with him."

In the Book of Timothy (2 Timothy 2:23–26), Paul exhorted Timothy to be kind to the believers who have fallen in the snares of the devil and are now under his influence, doing his will. They become captives; whereas, they used to be free in the past. They did something that led them to captivity again. This shows that Christians who are not prudent can fall into the snares of the devil and start doing his will.

The Book of Galatians mentioned (Galatians 3:1): "O foolish Galatians, who hath bewitched you, that ye should not obey the truth, before whose eyes Jesus Christ hath been evidently set forth, crucified among you." This proves that someone might know the truth and then be overpowered by another spirit and be brought back to the law and to regression.

Those in similar cases represent potential candidates for deliverance.

This concludes the discussion of the first component of deliverance, which is "The Teaching of Deliverance." It is not enough, however to know, understand, and teach deliverance. The anointing is greatly needed if one must operate deliverance.

Questionnaire

1. What have we been delivered from?

   _____

   _____

2. What is the meaning of the present deliverance?

   _____

   _____

3. What deliverance will God still perform to complete what He started?

   _____

   _____

4. What is the purpose of deliverance?

5. Is the transformation of the spirit of man progressive?

6. Is the transformation that affects the human soul (mind, emotions, will) and body instantaneous?

7. What responsibility must Christians take toward one another, especially toward the newly born ones?

8. What did Jesus do in the temple according to John 2:13–15?

9. What is the significance of Jesus' action in John 2:13–15 for the temple today?

_____

_____

10. What are the four types of people who benefit from deliverance?

_____

_____

Part 2

THE ANOINTING IN THE PRACTICE OF DELIVERANCE

In the process of deliverance, (1) it is paramount to depend upon the Holy Spirit, (2) it is important to know how to identify demons, and (3) to cast them out.

Chapter Three

Dependence upon the Holy Spirit

Jesus, in Matthew 12:28, reveals that dependence upon the Holy Spirit is the key for the anointing needed to identify demons and to cast them out: "But if I cast out devils by the Spirit of God, then the kingdom of God is come unto you." Then, in another context, He made it plain to His disciples how they can cast out any kind of demonic spirits. In fact, He was teaching them how to be dependent upon the Holy Spirit. Jesus, in Mark 8:14–29, indicated three factors that would qualify His disciples in the art of deliverance: a relationship with the Word of God, a life of prayer and fasting, and a compassion for the oppressed.

An Inner Familiarity with the Word of God

What Is the Word of God?

- The Word of God reveals God to man through Jesus Christ who is the Word and perfect image of God (John 1:1; Hebrews 1:1–2; Colossians 1:1–15).

- The Word of God is the source of Life (John 1:4; Psalm 119:93).
- The Word of God makes us grow spiritually (1 Peter 2:2). It is a spiritual food (Matthew 4:4).
- The Word of God is the source of salvation (Ephesians 1:13).
- The Word of God is the truth (John 8:32). It is the only thing that can free man from any kind of slavery: By reading and knowing the Word of God, a person can discover the dimensions of sin and slavery in his life and how Jesus can save him from it. The Word of God is the truth that sanctifies (John 17:17).
- The Word of God is the source of faith (Romans 10:17).
- The Word of God is a spiritually effective weapon for deliverance (Hebrews 4:12). It gives victory over Satan (1 John 2:14). It is the sword of the Spirit (Ephesians 6:17).

The Minister's Relationship with the Word of God

When His disciples were facing the case of deliverance they failed to solve, the first thing Jesus referred to was their lack of faith and the relationship between Him and His disciples: "O faithless generation, how long shall I be with you? How long shall I suffer you? Bring him unto me" (Mark 9:19). Jesus Himself, when confronting the devil in the wilderness, kept on saying: "It is written…" (Luke 4:4, 8, 12). In deliverance, it is supremely important to develop a faith based on the understanding of and obedience to the written Word of God. It must be expressed and strengthened through a relationship with the Living Word.

It is vital that the minister knows the Word of God. The minister must take the responsibility to study and get

Dependence upon the Holy Spirit

the knowledge of the written Word of God. The Word says: "But the Comforter, which is the Holy Ghost, whom the Father will send in my name, he shall teach you all things, and bring all things to your remembrance, whatsoever I have said unto you" (John 14:26).

The minister must store the Word of God. The word *remembrance* indicates that it is the minister's responsibility to get the Word of God richly dwelling in him for the Holy Spirit to bring it up to his remembrance when needed. That is the responsibility that expresses the seriousness of the minister concerning the ministry of deliverance. Knowledge of and obedience to the Word pleases the Holy Spirit who will enlighten the minister and reveal the truth to him when he is facing challenges. The Word of God is the principal equipment in the hand of the minister for discerning the spirits. God Himself has inspired the Word of God to men who transcribed it. That is why it is a necessity to read it currently and meditate upon it day and night (Joshua 1:8; Psalm 1:1–3; 2 Timothy 3:16).

The minister must submit to the Word of God. The ministry of deliverance must be infused and dominated by the Word of God. Since the Bible says that "ye shall know the truth and the truth shall set you free" (John 8:32), the deliverance minister, especially even more, should see that the Word of God infuses all aspects of deliverance. The authority and the substance of the Word of God must infuse the deliverance ministry. All other teaching or belief that is not in line with the Word of God must be excluded from the ministry.

What kind of relationship must the minister have with the Word of God? The minister of deliverance must seek to develop a relationship with the Word of God. A relationship with Jesus is effective through a life in the Word, for Jesus is the Word of God. An attachment to the Word of God in terms of meditation and obedience shows how much one is living and growing in one's relationship with the Lord Jesus. Jesus questioned His disciples saying how long should He remain for them to have this kind of relationship with Him and to manifest a faith that produces the fruit of deliverance. Such relationship is the means by which the minister can be equipped with the essential armor:

- A relationship that brings light. The minister will be full of the light that expels darkness, for "the entrance of thy words giveth light...." (Psalm 119:130a).
- A relationship that brings understanding. The minister will receive the spiritual understanding to deal with complicated situations, for "it (the entrance of thy words) giveth understanding unto the simple" (Psalm 119:130). Again "the Word of God is quick and powerful, sharper than any twoedged sword, piercing even to the dividing asunder of soul and spirit, and of the joints and marrow, and is a discerner of the thoughts and intents of the heart" (Hebrews 4:12).
- A relationship that brings authority. The minister will also operate at the level of the commanding authority that is above the universe; for God said, "so shall my word be that goes forth out of my mouth, it shall not return unto me void, it shall accomplish that which I please and it shall prosper in the thing whereto I sent it" (Isaiah 55:11).

A Life of Prayer and Fasting

Franklin Hall wrote: "Our ultimate aim and desire should be the exalting of Jesus Christ and the glorifying of Him. Without prayer and fasting every Christian will

DEPENDENCE UPON THE HOLY SPIRIT

more or less mark a time and fail in their purpose. The most successful and the quickest method is through prayer and fasting."[6]

What Is Prayer?

Man is the only creature that God made according to His own image. The reason is that God wanted to have communion with one of His creatures. Prayer is primarily communing with God. Therefore, God is the founder of prayer. The man Jesus exemplified the kind of relationship God has planned to have with man. His life was a life of prayer. Prayer was the key principle of His life and ministry. His thirst for the presence of His Father was what drove Him into regular withdrawing from the people, even from His disciples.

- Jesus' ministry was a direct result of His life of communion with His Father: "Verily, verily, I say unto you, the Son can do nothing of himself, but what he seeth the Father do; for whatsoever he doeth, these also doeth the Son likewise" (John 5:19).
- Jesus had the habit to get alone to pray: "And in the morning, rising up a great while before day, He went out, and departed into a solitary place, and there prayed" (Mark 1:35; see also 6:46; Matthew 14:23, 26:36; Luke 5:16, 9:28–29, 11:1; John 6:15).
- Jesus spent nights praying (Luke 6:12, 21:37).
- Jesus taught His disciples how to pray (Matthew 6:9–13).

---

[6] Franklin Hall, *Fasting: Atomic Power with God*, p.12.

- Jesus told them that through prayer they could break demonic resistance and cast them out (Mark 9:29; Matthew 17:21).
- Jesus told His disciples that His house should be a house of prayer for all nations (Mark 11:17; Matthew 21:13).
- Jesus encouraged them to pray (Matthew 21:22; Luke 18:1).
- Jesus commanded His disciples to wait (pray) for the promise of the Father (Acts 1:4).
- Jesus' prayer opened heaven (Luke 3:21).
- Jesus prayed for His disciples (Luke 22:32; John 17:1–26).
- Jesus prayed for all human souls' salvation (Luke 22:41, 44–45).
- Jesus prayed for the coming of the Holy Spirit (John14:16).

Jesus, through His life, is showing that the Christian life must be a life of prayer. How much more should it be for the deliverance minister? Therefore, it is not surprising that the enemy will be fighting, by all means, prayer in the lives of the children of God and prayer in the Church. Francis Frangipane said that "even lower attendance at prayer meetings will be used by the enemy to discourage even the most faithful from the position of prayer…We must not put down the sword."[7]

What Is Fasting?

Fasting is a spiritual exercise that consists of humbling ourselves before God, in total or partial abstinence of the desires of our flesh in order to dedicate our time to the

---

[7] Francis Frangipane, *The House of the Lord*, p.166.

spiritual development of our spirit man. The flesh/carnal desires could be food, drinks, sexual relations in marriage, sleep, comfort, speech (talking), pleasure, or leisure, etc.

Fasting, as in the pursuit of God's presence. Fasting has been and still is a serious issue in God's relationship with His people. God, before taking the children of Israel into the Promise Land, needed them to first check their hearts and make the needed adjustments that would allow them to become obedient to His Word. In the process through which God put them—before feeding them with the manna—fasting was one of the main disciplines that God forced the children of Israel to observe. This is what He said to them, "I humble thee and suffer thee to hunger" (Deuteronomy 8:3a). God, knowing that food is a great need of humankind, took the initiative of depriving His people of it. By suffering them to hunger, God put pressure on them to get them completely dependent on Him. Then, God brought the manna, not from the earth but from heaven, to get them to realize "We can rely on Him, He can take care of us, He is able." That is the way God chose to make His people know that "man doth not live by bread only, but by every word that proceedeth out of the mouth of the Lord, doth man live" (Deuteronomy 8:3b). God wants man to think like Him, in order that they may walk together and fulfill His purpose. But there are some things inside of man that can hinder the fulfillment of God's purpose.

As God's people, believers today must set aside time to pull themselves out of the daily routine of life so as to immerse themselves in the Word and receive some understanding of who God says in His Word that they are. When they see themselves in comparison to the Word, then godly sorrow and repentance can arise, leading to asking for mercy, forgiveness, and cleansing. Then God Himself will start making a change inside, bringing back the first love, the right attitude, conduct, and conversation. He will strengthen His people so as to make them determined to follow Him more than ever before.

Another thing that fasting will do is to help God's people to grow in communion with Him. By creating man in His own image, God expressed His desire to commune with Him. Since this communion happens most of the time in the period of fasting, fasting therefore appears as a means to satisfy the purpose of God.

Fasting as a way of humbling one's soul and dominating the creation. In fasting, humility comes by the fact that God destroys the power of self: God deals inside of His people to remove pride, selfish ambitions, and carnal passions. Everything that is their own and does not please God becomes weaker and weaker. God can do a new thing inside.

Fasting is also a means of taking dominion over creation. This is one of the aspects of fasting that Jesus also emphasized. Jesus said (in Mark 9:29) that fasting is one of the means (combined with prayer and meditation of the Word) to empower God's people to deal with the creation. Fasting will cause the anointing to come upon God's people and enable them to face the creation and rule over all the works of God's hand, the works that have been put under their feet (Psalm 8:4–6).

God's people are once more instructed to change their life of prayer and fasting. In the Book of Isaiah (chapter 58), God indicated the kind of fast He has chosen; meaning that God is so interested in fasting that He looked at different kinds of fasting and chose one. It is obvious that God will be pleased if His people do the fast He has chosen. The fast God has chosen includes the empowerment of His people to loose the oppressed, to set the captives free, to break the bands of wickedness, to be able to serve people properly

Dependence upon the Holy Spirit

with effectiveness not just with a contemplative compassion. Someone afflicted with HIV/AIDS will certainly appreciate it more if he or she is set free and healed than any other expression of compassion.

God expects His people to fast. Dr. Mary Ruth Swope wrote that "fasting opens our spiritual ears…the spirit gets stronger…the Holy Spirit can get His messages through easier…."[8]

> Jesus said: "Moreover when you fast, be not, as the hypocrites, of a sad countenance: for they disfigure their faces, that they may appear unto men to fast. Verily I say unto you, they have their reward. But thou, when thou fastest, anoint thine head, and wash thy face: that thou appear not unto men to fast, but unto thy Father which is in secret: and thy Father which seeth in secret, shall reward thee openly."
>
> (Matthew 6:16–17)

The Responsibility of the Minister of God

The Prerequisites

"Surely if man's scientific achievement has increased in momentum, there must also be something to be found somewhere in the Word of God that will accelerate his spiritual progress. Like most scriptural truths, there is something; but only the wise shall understand it. Its seemingly insignificance and misunderstanding of may be the cause for its neglect. This latent power is fasting and prayer."[9]

In the account of Mark (9:14–29), after Jesus had cast out the demon and obtained the deliverance of the young boy, His disciples asked Him privately, "Why could not we

---

[8] Mary R. Swope, *The Roots and Fruits of Fasting*, p.65.
[9] Franklin Hall, *Fasting: Atomic Power with God*, p.12.

cast him out?" (Mark 9:28). Jesus answered saying unto them: "This kind can come forth by nothing, but by prayer and fasting" (Mark 9:29).

Here, Jesus indicated that a life that combines praying with fasting as being one of the main conditions by which His disciples could become dependent upon the Holy Spirit. Jesus Himself, the Living Word of God, before confronting the devil after His baptism, had been led to the wilderness where He would wait upon His Father to endue Him with power while He emptied Himself through forty days of fasting: "And Jesus being full of the Holy Ghost returned from Jordan, and was led by the Spirit into the wilderness, being forty days tempted of the devil. And in those days he did eat nothing: and when they were ended, He afterward hungered" (Luke 4:1–2).

As Jesus did, it is through prayer and fasting that the minister can obtain mercy and grace to help the oppressed to be delivered.

Exercising His Responsibility

How can the minister obtain mercy from God for the oppressed souls? The minister must ask mercy from God for the soul to be delivered: "Let us therefore come boldly unto the throne of grace that we may obtain mercy, and find grace to help in time of need" (Hebrew 4:16). God even delights in receiving such prayers and will certainly answer them. That is why He said to come boldly before His throne. God insisted that His people come and ask. In James 4:2b God said, "yet ye have not, because ye ask not." Again "how much more shall your heavenly father give the Holy Spirit to them that ask Him?" (Luke 11:13).

How can the minister exercise authority? The minister must exercise authority over the enemy in warfare prayers

DEPENDENCE UPON THE HOLY SPIRIT

for the life of the victim. Once made captives, the only hope remaining for people is a deliverer (Luke 4:18). Many sheep remain captives and struggle under the oppression of evil spirits because no one is there to rescue them. Unless David fought the lion and the bear, the sheep could not escape once captured. Peter was able to escape while James perished. The difference was the intervention of someone else: the church in prayer and fasting (Acts 12).

How can the minister empty himself? How can one get filled with the presence of God, endued with His power, and burn with His fire unless he first mortifies self and gets its affections and lusts crucified? Through fasting and in prayer and the Word, the minister can get such a manifestation of God's power that chains are broken and captives set free: "Is not this the fast that I have chosen? To loose the bands of wickedness, to undo the heavy burdens, and to let the oppressed go free, and that ye break every yoke?" (Isaiah 58:6).

Questionnaire

1. How did Jesus cast out demons and how did He teach His disciples to prepare for it?

   _____

   _____

2. What is the basis for depending upon the Holy Spirit?

   _____

   _____

3. What are the main factors in developing a relationship with the Word of God?

4. Is it necessary to memorize the Word of God in order to grow?

5. How does one begin a relationship with the Word of God?

6. How does one grow in dependence upon the Holy Spirit?

7. How does fasting affect the flesh and the world?

8. Does God want His people to fast today?

DEPENDENCE UPON THE HOLY SPIRIT

9. How did Jesus teach His disciples concerning effectiveness and momentum in ministry?

_____

_____

10. What are the two main responsibilities of the minister toward the oppressed souls?

_____

_____

Chapter Four

IDENTIFYING DEMONS

Two fundamental questions help determine the means of identifying demons:

- What does the Word say about the Holy Spirit in terms of the operation of spiritual gifts in knowing the symptoms of demonic presence?
- What does the Word say about satanic spirits and the way they have access to a person's life and proceed to operate their destructive works?

In the light of these questions, the following approach has been adopted: Answering these questions leads us (1) to see how to use spiritual gifts to discern demonic presence, (2) to know more about Satan through the Word of God, and (3) to understand practical spiritual doors.

Operating in Spiritual Gifts to Discern the Symptoms of Demonic Presence

Spiritual Gifts in Deliverance

The spiritual gifts are useful equipment in deliverance. The revelation gifts, such as the gift of word of knowledge, help one to know the origins and the reasons of the case, while the gift of discerning of spirits exposes the spirit beings involved. Also, the power gifts, such as the gifts of faith, of healings, and of working of miracles, convey the power to cast out the evil spirits, destroy their works, and transform the situation.

Knowledge of the Symptoms of Demonic Presence

Demonic presence is often hidden. As in a laboratory, the use of appropriate tools can be helpful for a primary investigation (see attached a form for soul diagnosis). But all tools would be ineffective without the intervention of the Holy Spirit.

In the Case of Non-Obvious Signs of Demonic Presence

The presence of demons in one's life is often without obvious manifestations.

Without being a proof of demonic presence, certain specific behaviors such as those following can attract demonic presence or express it:

- Abnormal use of the tongue: Excess of words, lies, gossip, calumnies, false witness, criticism, foul language, and/or mean words, etc.
- Unbalanced behavior: violent anger, fights and the use of violence, quarrels, lack of forgiveness, jealousy, an inferiority or superiority complex,

exaggerated fear, feeling of not being loved, living in chaos or in filth, selfishness, and/or shyness.
- Recurrent situations without any evident cause and problems without physical reasons.

Watchman Nee stated: "Behind various difficulties are demons who actually hold the rein. If we are not watchful we may consider these to be purely human or physical difficulties. But if we have spiritual insight we will see through these hindrances and so cast out the demons who hide behind them."[10]

The Necessary Help of the Holy Spirit

"Howbeit when he, the Spirit of truth, is come, he will guide you into all truth: for he shall not speak of himself; but whatsoever he shall hear, that shall he speak: and he will show you things to come. He shall glorify me: for he shall receive of mine, and shall show it unto you" (John 16:13–14). The Holy Spirit will show us what is of God, allowing us also to know what isn't of God. Therefore, by the Spirit of God it is possible to discern demonic manifestations.

Knowing the Word of God Concerning Satan and His Demons

Elements Concerning Satan

Through deliverance, the Church comes to know practically him who is called Satan, his reality, and level of influence. Thus, through deliverance, the devil is demystified. The Lord says "fear not." By confronting the devil experimentally, the saints are strengthened in their faith; it is more than head knowledge: It is a reality that demons

---

[10] Watchman Nee, *The Prayer Ministry of the Church*, p.126.

cannot stand the sons of God: "And they were astonished at his doctrine for his word was with power. And in the synagogue there was a man, who had a spirit of an unclean devil, and cried out with a loud voice, saying, let us alone; what have we to do with thee, thou Jesus of Nazareth? Art thou come to destroy us? I know thee who thou art; the Holy One of God" (Luke 4:32–34). Even the devil flees in confrontation with the sons of God: "Submit yourselves therefore to God, Resist the devil and he will flee from you" (James 4:7).

Again, in the wilderness, when Jesus resisted him with the Word of God, the devil had no choice but to flee from Him: "And Jesus answered him saying it is written that man shall not live by bread alone, but by every word of God...Get thee behind me, Satan, for it is written: thou shalt worship the Lord thy God, and Him only shalt thou serve...It is said thou shalt not tempt the Lord thy God" (Luke 4:4, 8, 12).

Take note that in the account of Matthew, the Holy Spirit is the one who led Jesus into that confrontation. God desires that Christians realize that they have authority over all the forces of darkness. What Christians need to do is to stand on God's Word and to be led by the Spirit of God.

When we listen to those who have come from serving Satan, they always declare that Christians do not know what they have in terms of authority. That is why they are not bold enough in warfare when it comes to using their authority.

The Book of Matthew says that the kingdom of God suffers violence: "And from the days of John the Baptist until now the Kingdom of heaven suffereth violence, and the violent take it by force" (Matthew 11:12). The kingdom of God can only advance through conflict. There is an antagonism in the nature of the kingdom of God that opposes the kingdom of darkness. There cannot be any negotiation.

The kingdom of God must push back the kingdom of darkness in order to progress. There is an antagonism between the two kingdoms. There is no area of concession, collaboration, or conciliation. It is a continual conflict between the two kingdoms. The only way to make the kingdom of God advance is to push back and destroy the kingdom of darkness.

The Bible says that there is a special kind of Christian: the Christians who are violent in the spirit, those who do not compromise or negotiate the kingdom of God. These are those who use their spiritual authority and the Holy Spirit power to transform lives and advance the kingdom. Their spirit is on fire and releases the fire of the Holy Spirit to push back the kingdom of darkness.

Unfortunately, many Christians have not reached this point of authority. The Lord is a man of war (Exodus 15:3). By nature Christians are warriors; they must be violent in spirit, the God-kind of violence against the devil. All Christians must know how God dealt with Satan and imitate God.

    A. Satan as a created being

        First of all, the reality of Satan should not be exaggerated to cause people to fear; also, it should not be underestimated to make people forget it and even pretend that the devil does not exist. It is healthy to bring the right measure of spiritual reality concerning the enemy.

        Satan is a creature. He was created at a certain point in time. He is not the creator. He can never be God. A creature can never become God. Only God is

Creator: "Thou hast been in Eden the garden of God; every precious stone was thy covering, the sardius, topaz, and the diamond, the beryl, the onyx, and the jasper, the sapphire, the emerald, and the carbuncle, and gold: the workmanship of thy tabrets and of thy pipes was prepared in thee in the day that thou wast created" (Ezekiel 28:13).

B. His perfection was not apart from God

Satan was not created as Satan. His name was Lucifer at his creation: "How art thou fallen from heaven, O Lucifer...." (Isaiah 14:12). God created him perfect: "Thou was perfect in thy ways from the day that thou wast created, till iniquity was found in thee" (Ezekiel 28:15). Satan is a creature and he can never be God. As a creature, he was the result of God's work. That is why at his creation as Lucifer he was perfect. The perfection he had received as Lucifer was not a perfection of himself but it was a perfection in reflecting from the holy mountain of God the beauty of the light of God (Ezekiel 28:14).

C. Creation through the Son of God

All things were created through the only begotten Son of God, Jesus. It is written that all things were created through the Word and nothing was created without the Word, meaning without going through Jesus (John 1:1–14). Again in the Book of Colossians the same truth is confirmed: "for by Him (Jesus) were all things created, that are in heaven, and that are in earth, visible and invisible, whether they be thrones, or dominions, or principalities, or powers; all things were created by Him, and for Him: and He

IDENTIFYING DEMONS

is before all things, and by Him all things consist" (Colossians 1:16–17).

God the Father, God the Son Jesus, and God the Holy Spirit is the only One God Creator. And God says to not be afraid, meaning that Christians should walk with Him, the Creator, who holds all things by the word of His power and not be afraid of any creation, fallen ones or not.

D. His position of beauty

The position given by God to Lucifer at his creation had allowed him to manifest some beauty (Ezekiel 28:12, 14). Lucifer did not have that beauty apart from God. In fact, the Lord had put all the precious stones upon Lucifer to just be a reflecting instrument of the light of God. As long as Lucifer was positioned where God placed him to reflect the light of Jesus, just as the moon reflects the sun, he was in the right place.

E. Pride brought about Lucifer's fall to become Satan

The reason for the fall was pride; Lucifer had his heart lifted up because of his beauty. Instead of giving glory to God, Lucifer thought the glory he had was his own, but it was only the reflection of the light of Jesus passing through him: "Thine heart was lifted up because of thy beauty, thou hast corrupted thy wisdom by reason of thy brightness" (Ezekiel 28:17).

F. His attempt to implement what pride conceived in him

He tried to ascend into heaven, to rule over the stars and the angels; he tried to receive glory from the congregation. He tried to take the glory from God, something that did not belong to him. He tried to have a position that was not his (Isaiah 14:13).

G. How God dealt with the rebel and the rebellion

God was radical and violent in dealing with Satan and his demons. God basically said that when He finished dealing with Satan those who had known him would not recognize him anymore. They would be astonished upon seeing the terror of yesterday brought to naught: "I will cast thee to the ground, I will lay thee before kings, that they may behold thee. Thou hast defiled thy sanctuaries by the multitude of thine iniquities, by the iniquity of thy traffick; therefore will I bring forth a fire from the midst of thee, it shall devour thee, and I will bring thee to ashes upon the earth in the sight of all them that behold thee. All they that know thee among the people shall be astonished at thee: thou shalt be a terror, and never shalt thou be any more" (Ezekiel 28:17b–19).

Again, God pronounced violent judgment upon Satan in the Book of Isaiah: "how thou art fallen from heaven…how art thou cut down to the ground, which did weaken the nations…yet thou shalt be brought down to hell, to the sides of the pit…they that see thee shall narrowly look upon thee, and consider thee, saying is this the man that made the earth to tremble, that did shake kingdoms, that made the world as a wilderness that destroyed the cities thereof; that opened not the house of his prisoners?…but thou art cast out of thy grave like an abominable branch…." (Isaiah 14:12–19).

Identifying Demons

In the Book of Revelation, all of God's dealings are expressed in terms of war in heaven: "And there was a war in heaven; Michael and his angels fought against the dragon, and the dragon fought and his angels, and prevailed not; neither was their place found anymore in heaven. And the great dragon was cast out, that old serpent, called the devil and Satan, which deceiveth the whole world: he was cast out into the earth, and his angels were cast out with him" (Revelation 12:7–9).

The kind of spirit that animated God in dealing with Satan and his demons is the violent spirit that takes the kingdom of God by force. Christians need to receive the impartation of that violence in their spirits in dealing with the forces of darkness. In heaven there has been a lot of casting out. This is the way to deal with Satan and his demons: cast them out. This is the way if it is to be done with them on earth just as it has been done with them in heaven (Matthew 6:10).

As for Satan, he realizes (even more than certain Christians do) that he does not have all powers; he has been given some power, given some beauty, given some wisdom, but it is all corrupted. Also, it is clear that Satan is not omniscient: he does not know everything; he is not omnipresent: he cannot be everywhere at the same time; and he is not omnipotent: he does not have all power. As a matter of fact, Christians have more power than him because "greater is He that is in us than he who is in the world" (1 John 4:4). So why would a child of God be afraid of Satan and how much less his demons?

Jesus promised that Christians would cast them out in His name (Mark 16:17).

Elements Concerning Demons

When Satan and his demons fell from heaven they continued their evil activities in the high places (second heaven), on the earth, and in the seas. From these places they oppress, obsess, and possess humans, animals, and places:

- Demonic actions against men (Luke 11:24–26); against animals (Mark 5:11–13); demonic actions in certain places: high places (Ephesians 2:1–2, 6:12); places on the surface of the earth, in the sea (Revelation 12:12, Isaiah 27:1, the Leviathan); in hell (the dwelling place of Satan and demons before the lake of fire) where some of them are already imprisoned (2 Peter 2:4).

  A. Origin, number, organization of demons

  They are the angels that Satan brought with him in his fall (Revelation 12:7–9; Isaiah 14:12–17). They were about one-third of the angels (Revelation 12:3–4). Satan is their chief. They are organized in principalities, powers, rulers of darkness, and spiritual wickedness (Ephesians 6:12).

  B. Objectives of demons

  Demons fight against God (Daniel 10:2–6, 12–14, 20–21). For example, God's answer to Daniel was delayed by demonic attacks: "Then said he unto me, Fear not, Daniel: for from the first day that thou didst set thine heart to understand, and to chasten thyself before thy God, thy words were heard, and I am come for thy words. But the prince of the kingdom of Persia withstood me one and twenty days: but, lo, Michael, one of the chief princes, came to help me; and I remained there with the kings of Persia."

Demons fight against men. They want to kill men: "The thief cometh not, but for to steal, and to kill, and to destroy: I am come that they might have life, and that they might have it more abundantly" (John 8:44, 10:10).

They want to submit men to their will: "And that they may recover themselves out of the snare of the devil, who are taken captive by him at his will" (2 Timothy 2:25–26).

They try to make men revolt against God through unbelief and false doctrines: "For the time will come when they will not endure sound doctrine; but after their own lusts shall they heap to themselves teachers, having itching ears; And they shall turn away their ears from the truth, and shall be turned unto fables" (2 Timothy 4:3–4).

They attack Christians and create trouble so that the gospel will not be proclaimed or preached (Revelation 2:10; Acts 16:16–24, 17:13–14).

C. Mode of demonic operation

Demons exercise their actions on men mainly through possession, obsession, and oppression:

- Possession

It is the action by which Satan and his demons establish their throne in the spirit of man and then take complete control of him. It seems like a system of autosuggestion keeps the person repeating to himself the kinds of thoughts that have been programmed in him (Luke 8:26–29, 33, 9:38–39). The same manifestations are reproduced at regular intervals: every hour, every night, or permanently. Each time there is a submission to Satan and his demons they will try to entirely possess the individual. This case can also occur when, at birth or conception of pregnancy, the life of the fetus was offered to Satan; or when the parents consulted a magician, witchcraft, or water spirits (for example). The gospel must be preached to them, for Satan is trying to steal that which is not his: "Thine eyes did see my substance, yet being unperfect; and in thy book all my members were written, which in continuance were fashioned, when as yet there was none of them" (Psalm 139:16).

- Obsession

It is the action through which the unclean spirit imposes on the thoughts of the person, independently of his will, a fixed idea of sin, so that the person will be obliged to come back to it unceasingly. It is the case of sexually addicted persons, "crack" smokers, alcoholic persons, etc.

- Oppression

It is the action by which the satanic spirits have partial right on man. They exercise their right on different frequencies: either on one part of the body or on the whole body. The frequency of the oppression can be: periodical, i.e. the sufferings stop and come back at intervals of time or according to circumstances.

IDENTIFYING DEMONS

D. How Satan and his demons proceed to get doors open

Consciously or unconsciously man can fall into the trap of Satan and remain under his power (Hosea 4:6). Derek Prince said: "No limit can be set to the forms of deception practiced in the occult. As soon as one is exposed, another emerges in its place. It is therefore impossible to give a complete or definitive list of the various types of occult practices. It is, however, possible to identify and briefly describe the following three main branches: witchcraft, divination and sorcery:

- Witchcraft is the power branch of the occult. It is the expression of man's rebellion against God (1 Samuel 15:23). Its driving force is a desire to control people and circumstances. To gain this end, it manipulates, intimidates, or dominates.

- Divination (see further)

- Sorcery (see further)

Satan and his demons need to have an open door in order to gain access to a life. They use any kind of trick to tempt and push man so to get these doors open. Once they get the access they bind the person and exercise their actions. Devices are means that Satan uses in his attempt to push someone to act or react in a way that a door might be opened. Satan and his demons are very active especially in getting doors open in the lives of those who preach the Gospel. Dr. G. Greenwald said that over and over he has observed seducing spirits assigned to bring about the downfall of Christian leaders. Most pastors, whether married or single, can usually tell horror stories of women who have literally thrown themselves at them. Those leaders do not have to be physically good-looking, charming, or even financially well-off. The women being used to bring their downfall are actually driven by seducing spirits who have been assigned to attempt to stop the preaching of the Gospel. Satan knows he cannot attack those men unless he can get them to break their own hedge of protection.[11]

God's Hedge of Protection Is Sure

God has put a hedge of protection around every human. That hedge prevents the devil from gaining access to man and destroying him at his will. That is why Satan complained before God in the case of Job: "Hast not thou made an hedge about him, and about his house, and about all that he hath on every side?" (Job 1:10a). Unless the hedge is broken, Satan cannot perform his actions. The same truth is expressed in the Book of Ecclesiastes: "He that diggeth a pit shall fall into it; and whoso breaketh an hedge, a serpent shall bite him" (Ecclesiastes 10:8). The serpent (who is Satan) would like to bite, but he cannot do it until someone opens a door to his life.

A door is therefore an access into an area of one's life for demonic spirits to come in and work destruction. It takes someone who will break the hedge. Satan cannot provide himself access to one's life by breaking the hedge, he has to get someone to do it.

How Is the Hedge Broken?

The hedge is broken by walking in disobedience, by having unrepented sin, by living in the flesh: "There is therefore

---

[11] Dr. Gary L Greenwald, *Seductions Exposed*, p.97.

now no condemnation to them which are in Christ Jesus, who walk not after the flesh, but after the Spirit" (Romans 8:1). This absence of condemnation is for the believers who walk after the Spirit, but there is condemnation for those who walk after the flesh: they break the hedge of protection and the serpent can bite them. Neil T. Anderson said: "You are no longer compelled to walk according to the flesh as you were before conversion. And now you are not even compelled to walk according to the Spirit. You are completely free to choose to walk according to the Spirit or to walk according to the flesh."[12]

That is why God keeps on exhorting His people to walk after the Spirit by living in obedience to the Word of God. Obedience is a way to remain under God's protection and blessings.

Man can disobey by himself. In the case of demonic oppression, demons often get man to disobey and open doors by attacking him at the level of his mind. They suggest ideas to man without allowing him to know that these ideas come from them. They want man to continue to believe that the ideas are his. These ideas can be arguments and reasoning, opposed to the Word of God, which allows man to justify himself while he needs to repent. That is why all thoughts must be examined and submitted to the authority of the Lord Jesus Christ (2 Corinthians 10:3–5).

Generational or Personal Doors

- Doors can be generational
  These are openings at the level of previous generations (the parents, grandparents, great-grandparents, and great-great-grandparents): idolatry, sexual immorality, witchcraft, altars, covenants, sacrifices,

---
[12] Neil T. Anderson, *Victory over the Darkness*, p.101.

pacts, oaths, magic, divination, and sects.[13] These are doors that the enemy can use to operate (Exodus 20:1–5).

- Doors can also be personal

    These are openings at the individual level: personal iniquities including curses, soul ties, and former relationships, which have not really been severed, are doors at a personal level that the enemy can use.

- Examples of doors found in born-again Christians' lives

    a. "Occult background of the family: this may be unknown to oneself, but this (iniquity) still opens one to evil spirits of witchcraft, divination, and sorcery even if not personally involved.
    b. Personal occultic involvement: this is personal involvement in the use of charms, love potions, reading stars (horoscopes), palm reading, yoga, karate, etc. It is seeking for supernatural protection or provision.
    c. Signing of covenants and dedication to false deities, attending séances (spiritist meetings), and cults. Some traditional practices and cultures are highly demonic.
    d. Watching bad films and reading evil books, pictures, and filthy magazines of pornography and the like.
    e. Backsliding: No born-again Christian comes back the same after backsliding. Usually demons get into them. God in His wisdom, provided a way out, even for a backslider."[14]

---

[13] Derek Prince, *They Shall Expel Demons*, p.104.

Identifying Demons

Understanding Practical Spiritual Doors

The Spiritual Doors of Idolatry

> After He had taken the children of Israel out of the Egyptian bondage God spake to them saying: "I am the Lord thy God, which have brought thee out of the land of Egypt, out of the house of bondage. Thou shalt have no other gods before me. Thou shalt not make unto thee any graven image, or any likeness of any thing that is in heaven above, or that is in the earth beneath, or that is in the water under the earth: thou shalt not bow down thyself to them, nor serve them: for I the Lord thy God am a jealous God, visiting the iniquity of the fathers upon the children unto the third and fourth generation of them that hate me; and shewing mercy unto thousands of them that love me, and keep my commandments."
>
> (Exodus 20:1–6)

God first introduced Himself to the children of Israel as being the one who delivered them from the house of bondage. It was not by mistake that He identified Himself to them. God wanted them to have Him alone as their God. The first commandment God gave them was explicit: they should have no other gods before Him. Then God explained to them what He meant by not having other gods before Him. All these explanations were to show how serious He is about idolatry. God made it clear to His people that idolatry is provocation to Him because He is by nature a jealous God. To persuade them to turn from idolatry or not practice it, God made His people know the punishment reserved for idolaters and the reward for those who would worship Him alone and obey His commandments. God indicated that the punishment would not only affect those who disobeyed, but

---

[14] Mwanaliti Stephen, *Deliverance for the Delivered*, p.19.

even their descendants would suffer. By these punishments and rewards God is saying that unless this first commandment about idolatry is observed no other obedience will really count in His eyes. God means that the observance of the nine other commandments has no value at all until the first one is obeyed.

Since God reveals Himself (Father, Son, Holy Spirit) to man through His Son, Jesus Christ, obedience to this first commandment can only be genuine if one has accepted Jesus as personal Lord and Savior and the authority of the Bible as the infallible Word of God. Any other approach of God and worship of God is idolatry that is not based on who Jesus is according to the Bible:

> For great is the LORD, and greatly to be praised: he also is to be feared above all gods. For all the gods of the people are idols: but the LORD made the heavens.
> (1Chronicles 16:25–26)

> The children gather wood, and the fathers kindle the fire, and the women knead their dough, to make cakes to the queen of heaven, and to pour out drink offerings unto other gods, that they may provoke me to anger.
> (Jeremiah 7:18)

> Their idols are silver and gold, the work of men's hands. They have mouths, but they speak not: eyes have they, but they see not: They have ears, but they hear not: noses have they, but they smell not…They that make them are like unto them; so is every one that trusteth in them. O Israel, trust thou in the LORD: he is their help and their shield…."

To bow before statues is idolatry: "Then shall it be for a man to burn: for he will take thereof, and warm himself;

yea, he kindleth it, and baketh bread; yea, he maketh a god, and worshippeth it; he maketh it a graven image, and falleth down thereto."

(*)

Understanding Other Practical Doors

Sacrifices

This is an offering for satanic spirits by way of traditional or mystical rituals: the sacrifice can be immolation of a person, animal, or bird. Many families bring their children into bondage by giving them food sacrificed to idols (1 Corinthians 10:18–20). Anytime anything is being sacrificed on an altar, a powerful covenant comes into being.[15]

Oath

It is a formal promise made to the satanic spirits to sacrifice or dedicate children, offspring, or possessions. It could be the adoption of certain taboo. Example: Oath binding a woman to death if she cheats, etc.

Pact

It is an agreement established between persons or between persons and satanic spirits to dedicate children, offspring, spouses, or even any other person to these satanic spirits by way of a secret, traditional, or occult ceremony. It could also be money that is thrown to be picked up by someone or even gifts, etc.

(* see also 1 Thessalonians 1:1–9; 1 John 5:2–5)
[15] Olukoya D.K. *Release from Destructive Covenants*. #

Familiar Objects

They are objects that demons attach themselves to. Everything (objects) that is used for Satan's service represents a legal ground for demons to attach themselves to. Another type of familiar objects is the one satanists invoke demons upon and attach them to. These objects initially are not occult objects. After demons have been attached to them, they are offered as gifts to people that place them in their houses. These demons are responsible for bringing quarrels, fights between spouses, heaviness to pray or meditate on the Word of God, etc. Derek Prince said that "Sorcery operates through material objects or through other ways of impacting the physical senses, such as drugs and music."[16]

Sexual Immorality

- Homosexuality
  Although this word is defined as an erotic activity with another of the same sex, it is used here to designate sexual intercourse between two men. (Romans 1:27; Leviticus 18:22, 20:13)
- Lesbianism
  It is sexual relationship between women (Romans 1:26).
- Bestiality
  It is sexual intercourse between humans and animals (Exodus 22:19; Leviticus 18:23, 20:16).
- Masturbation
  It is the act of dishonoring one's own body with one's fingers.
- Incest
  It is the practice of sexual intercourse between family members (Leviticus 18:18, 20:11–12, 14, 17, 19–20;

---

[16] Derek Prince, *Blessing or Curse*, p.68.

IDENTIFYING DEMONS

1 Corinthians 5:1–5). For example: Lot and his two daughters (Genesis 19:31–34), king David's two children (2 Samuel 13:14), Absalom with his father's (king David's) two wives (2 Samuel 16:22).

- Adultery: sexual intercourse with a partner that is not the spouse. That is forbidden for both partners (Hebrews 13:4; Matthew 5:27–28). Jesus said in Matthew 5:27–28: "But I say unto you, That whosoever looketh on a woman to lust after her hath committed adultery with her already in his heart." Therefore, one must bring into captivity every thought to the obedience of Christ (2 Corinthians 10:5).
- Fornication: in a general sense, all forms of sexual immorality. In a specific way, it is sex before marriage. It is not permissible to have sexual relations before getting married—boys or girls. Even the engaged persons are not allowed to do so, that is why it is recommended for an engaged couple not to meet too many times alone (1 Thessalonians 4:3–4; 1 Corinthians 6:15–20).
- Perverted sexual practices: sodomy, oral sex, sex gadgets, and orgy (Romans 1:24–27).
- Divorce: breaking a marriage covenant (Malachi 2:13–16; Mark 10:4–12). Divorce is authorized only in the case of adultery (Matthew 19:3–9).
- Illegal union, with no engagement, or same blood marriage: these kinds of marriages should be broken also, in cases where one partner is an unbeliever (1 Corinthians 7:12–16).

These immoral sexual practices open doors for demons that come as "night husbands" (incubus sexual demon) or "night wives" (succubus sexual demon).

A. Night Husbands (incubus sexual demons)

Incubus is "an evil spirit that lies on a person in their sleep, one that has sexual intercourse with women while they are sleeping."

These kinds of demons possess women or young girls as a consequence of masturbation, pornographic movies, adultery, sodomy, orgy, incest, and sexual intercourse before marriage, use of sex gadgets, rape.

Even within the Christian marriage, impure sexual practices such as oral sex or sodomy give demons an open door into the lives of the couple. In the case of a couple, if one of the spouses is not yet a believer, the spouse who is a believer must refrain from such practices and ask God to sanctify the marital bed before sexual intercourse. The spouse who is a Christian must pray (according to 1 Corinthians 7:12–16) and must close every open door with the blood of Jesus so that no demons can infiltrate during sexual intercourse. The same prayer must be prayed in the case of a spouse who practices occultism.

Even virgin women can also be oppressed by demons if they practice "Carine games": touching other girls (in schools, dormitories, etc.).

There are serious consequences for practicing sexual immorality and opening doors for the entrance of the incubus sexual demon in the life of a woman. Some of these consequences are as follow:

- A woman oppressed by this kind of demon can become frigid in her marriage.

IDENTIFYING DEMONS

- Demons suggest immoral thoughts to draw one into sexual immorality and adultery.
- These demons will attack the children of the victim and sometimes bring death among her children.
- They sometimes attack the spouse with sexual impotency.
- The victim can sometimes see herself raped at night.
- The demons can make "masks of oldness" manifest on the face of the oppressed women in order to keep them in celibacy.

These kinds of demons usually leave without too much resistance once they are exposed.

B. Night Wives (succubus sexual demons)

Succubus are "demons assuming female form to have sexual intercourse with men in their sleep." This kind of demon oppresses men as a consequence of homosexuality, masturbation, rape, sexual intercourse before marriage, incest etc.

There are serious consequences for practicing sexual immorality and opening doors for the entrance of the succubus sexual demon in the life of a man. Some of these consequences are as follow:

- They can make the man impotent in his marriage.
- They can bring the man to sexual misconduct: that is why even in Christian couples some spouses cannot respect the rules of fasting (1 Corinthians 7:5).

- Night wives and night husbands are very jealous, so they create instability in couples and provoke separation and even divorce.

These kinds of demons (night wives) also leave without resistance after the doors by which they enter are exposed and they are cast out in the name of Jesus.

All demons can enter in people's lives through incantations, especially the spirit of the "queen of the waters" or the "queen of heaven."

In conclusion: Sexual immorality can bring physical and spiritual death. It is an open door to sexually transmissible diseases such as AIDS; it also opens doors to demons. It brings hereditary problems: Children whose parents were living in sexual disorder can struggle with ties of immodesty. For example, King Solomon, who had seven hundred wives and three hundred concubines, was born out of a union that was originally adulterous between King David and Bathsheba. Even children who are born of a polygamist marriage or outside of a marriage are born with some ties. For example, Ishmael, who was born of an illegal union between Abraham and Hagar, is the ancestor of Mohammed, whose religion accepts polygamy (Genesis 16:15).

Open Doors During Childhood[17]

Demons make a big effort to contact children at a very young age:

- There are toys, cartoons, and TV shows that aim to make children sensitive to the satanic spiritual world.

---

[17] Lester Sumrall, *Alien Entities*, p.65–70.

- Rape and incest in a child's life will bring infiltration of some of the most powerful demons, who will push their victims to self-destruction by way of suicide.
- Cursing a child, especially by his own parent, brings a curse into his life and is an open door for demons.
- Children who were not desired by their parents are born with an inner wound that is an open door to demons, especially the spirit of rejection.
- A family that lives under stress, divided, and unstable is vulnerable to the influence of demons on both parents and children.
- Some children are consecrated to satanic forces at birth because of the rituals that were practiced at their birth.
- Some families present their children to idols instead of presenting them to the Lord.
- At the birth of their child, some people give blood from their child to an occultist. This will allow the occultist or even Satan to possess the child. Spirits will establish themselves into the child's life and will control his personality and life. The child may notice that he has power or extraordinary abilities that cannot be explained. All these open doors lead to spiritual bondage.

Spiritual Bondage (as a Result of Spiritual Doors)

Definition: spiritual bondage is a spiritual state that is imposed in a person's life to keep him in sin and in its consequences. Once demons find their way into one's life, they establish bondages. There are many different kinds of bondages depending on the doors that demons have used. Here are some of those ways that may be the most ignored or neglected.

Bondage of Name Ties

A name somehow influences one's life and mission. Examples: Eve (Genesis 3:20), Abraham (Genesis 35:10–12), Jesus (Matthew 1:21). The characteristics of a name that give this influence are:

- The mystery that accompanied one's birth,
- The context in which the name was given,
- The spiritual state of the person whose name was given,
- The rituals that were performed at the ceremony when the name was given.

All these elements behind a name give the name its spiritual influence upon one's life. That is why every name must be sanctified by the blood of Jesus or changed. The Bible mentions a large repertoire of names of people who walked in faithfulness with the Lord and whose example of faith we are exhorted to follow (Hebrews 13:7).

Bondage of Family Ties

The family is a project of God. God is at the origin of all the families on Earth (Genesis 1:28). God blessed Adam and Eve and granted them an offspring. Through Abraham, God promised to bless all the families of the earth (Genesis 12:3). God also expects a family to be raised according to His ways (Genesis 18:18–19). God extends the same blessing to the earth through Isaac (Genesis 26:4).

At creation, God created the first couple and gave them the means and rights to: build a family (Genesis 2:24), give life (Genesis 1:27–28), and organize the environment for the well-being of the family (Genesis 2:15). God gave this couple the authority and the spiritual, moral, and physical power over the family. When man sinned, he became subjected to Satan and gave him the authority and the power that God had granted him (Romans 5:12–21). Since then, Satan has power over the offspring of men to steal, kill, and destroy (John10:10). Satan targets the family (cell) to introduce death in the world.

Families are the targets of the enemy. Parents who abandon their spiritual authority over their children are to a certain extent giving them over to Satan. By refusing to take their responsibilities and exercise their authority in raising their children in God's ways, the entire family comes under bondage.

Bondage of Soul Ties

Through sexual intercourse God allows soul ties in the context of marriage to strengthen the union. That is why God said that the two will become one flesh: "Therefore shall a man leave his father and mother, and shall cleave unto his wife: and they shall be one flesh" (Genesis 2:24). The devil has perverted the area of sexuality introducing all kinds of violations to God's command. As a result, ungodly soul ties are developed outside of marriage. Frank Hammond said that: "through sexual relationships outside of marriage, demonic soul ties are forged."[18] And people who fall into them are bound and suffer spiritually (demonic oppressions, bondages, curses, sexual nightmares, and fantasies); mentally (sexual flashback, perversion, no peace but torment); emotionally (fragmentation, instability, unsatisfactory); physically (sicknesses and diseases); etc.

---

[18] Frank Hammond, *Soul Ties*, p.3.

Vito Rallo said that, because of the soul tie, in case of separation with the partner or divorce, the "hurt turns to anger, then to resentment and bitterness."[19]

Bondage of Hereditary Ties

Every pact or idolatry in the family gives a legal ground for satanic oppressions over the offspring.

Their consequences are extended from the person who practices these sins up to the fourth generation (Exodus 20:3–5). These ties and curses will be transmitted from generation to generation. God planted a seed for reproduction by which each seed yields after its kind (Genesis 1:12). Spiritual ties obey the same law. That is why parents who are bound give birth to children who will also be bound.

For example, Achan was cursed by his actions and so was his wife and children even though they did not sin (Joshua 7:19–25). Moabites and Ammonites, of an incestuous relationship between Lot and his two daughters, all disappeared from the surface of the earth (Genesis 19:30–38). The Ammonites were spiritually tied by the curse of Lot and his two daughters (Isaiah 16:14; Ezekiel 25:1–11).

Bondage of Persons Ties

This is bondage caused by the influence of an occult person who lives with people or is around them at work. For example, a nurse who practices the occult has an influence on the newborn that she has in her charge.

Bondage of Sect Ties

A sect arises from a knowledge that they claim to have, which is different from, or deviates from Bible doctrine.

---

[19] Vito Rallo, *Breaking Generational Curses and Pulling down Strongholds*, p.144.

A sect brings together a group of disciples following the same master or sharing the same religious or philosophical beliefs.

Author of sects. Satan is the author of all sects. He continues to create sects to imitate the work of God (1 Timothy 4:1–3). He uses the following elements:

- Many people are in search of a religion that can give them a god of a material nature.
- When people are facing issues (sickness, sterility, misery, etc.), they often seek promises that will give an instant solution to their problems.

How to discern a sect. Initially, sects were religious groups spreading doctrines that were different from doctrines of other fundamentalist churches. Nowadays, many sects resemble closely the truth; even when they deviate from the truth it is difficult for the unknowing person to recognize them. The Bible says in Matthew 24:24: "For there shall arise false Christs, and false prophets, and shall shew great signs and wonders; insomuch that, if it were possible, they shall deceive the very elect." Nevertheless, we should not reject all those who do miracles and wonders as false Christs or false prophets nor call sect any religious group that has a different interpretation on a minor point of doctrine.

Here are some elements to help discern a sect:

- Some sects deny the divinity of Jesus and that God is His Father, even though the biblical message demonstrates it: "And we know that the Son of God is come, and hath given us an understanding, that we may know him that is true, and we are in him that is true, even in his Son Jesus Christ. This is the true God, and eternal life" (1 John 5:20; Hebrews 1:8). Some sects present a person as the savior of the world who they declare to be superior or equal to Jesus Christ. But the Bible says that salvation is only in Jesus: "Neither is there salvation in any other: for there is none other name under heaven given among men, whereby we must be saved" (Acts 4:12).

- Some sects say that the mission of their messiah is different from Jesus' work. The work of their messiah is presented as completing the mission of Jesus. The Bible says in many instances that all is fulfilled in Christ, especially the work that the Father had given Jesus to do: "These words spake Jesus, and lifted up his eyes to heaven, and said, Father, the hour is come; glorify thy Son, that thy Son also may glorify thee: As thou hast given him power over all flesh, that he should give eternal life to as many as thou hast given him. And this is life eternal, that they might know thee the only true God, and Jesus Christ, whom thou hast sent. I have glorified thee on the earth: I have finished the work which thou gavest me to do" (John 17:1–4).

- For other sects, the instrument of liberation and purification of men is something different than the cross and the blood of Jesus. The Bible says in Romans 6:6: "Knowing this, that our old man is crucified with him, that the body of sin might be destroyed, that henceforth we should not serve sin" (see also Hebrews 9:13–14; Revelation 1:5–6; 1 John 1:9).

- Some sects present external rules or sexual practices contrary to the Bible, for example: sexual relationship between couples, polygamy, etc.

IDENTIFYING DEMONS

Bondage of Bewitchment

This is the operation by which incantations are made on an image, a doll representing a person to whom harm is done or wounds are made to make the person suffer through occultism. Sometimes the image of the person is brought through a crystal ball, a bucket of water, a mirror, etc., upon which incantations are made.

These incantations can reach a Christian if he has open doors that enter in conflict with a bewitcher.

God forbids the practice of bewitchment: "There shall not be found among you any one that maketh his son or his daughter to pass through the fire, or that useth divination, or an observer of times, or an enchanter, or a witch. Or a charmer, or a consulter with familiar spirits, or a wizard, or a necromancer" (Deuteronomy 18:10–11).

Bondage of Magic

This is the production, by using incantations and the help of unclean spirits, of things contrary to the law of nature. These spirits that the magicians call upon are considered as beings that went through a certain transformation that is part of the process of reincarnation. The magicians also use books of incantations, bewitched objects, medals, rings, belts, bronze bracelets, and more. There are three different types of magic. Satanists often present magic as a science that opens the intelligence (Genesis 3:1–6).

- White magic: For uninitiated persons, white magic is "for the good of people." It is used to get—through unclean spirits—protection, luck, success, riches, professional promotion, healing, pregnancy, marriage, etc. Healers also use white magic to obtain healing for their patients.

- Black magic: Contrary to white magic, black magic is the one that is supposed to be for the evil. It is used to murder, to make people sick, to destroy people's possessions, businesses, jobs, etc.
- Red magic: Red magic is used to perpetrate actions at a large scale. For example: massacres, natural catastrophes that kill a great number of people by: airplane, boat, train accidents, and other forms of incidents.

Magic is condemned by God: "There shall not be found among you any one that maketh his son or his daughter to pass through the fire, or that useth divination, or an observer of times, or an enchanter, or a witch. Or a charmer, or a consulter with familiar spirits, or a wizard, or a necromancer. For all that do these things are an abomination unto the LORD: and because of these abominations the LORD thy God doth drive them out from before thee (Deuteronomy 18:10–12).

Bondage of Divination

It is predicting the unknown and the future. At the base of divination is a malefic power given to a person by unclean spirits, which gives the person the ability to see things (also called sixth sense) and perceive hidden things. This ability to see things is an imitation of the gift of prophecy that the Holy Spirit gives to Christians. The bewitcher uses objects that do not have any power by themselves but behind which Satan hides. It is through these objects that Satan manifests his tricks (i.e. mirror, bucket of water, mask, etc.). God condemns divination: "For these nations, which thou shalt possess, hearkened unto observers of times, and unto diviners: but as for thee, the LORD thy God hath not suffered thee so to do" (Deuteronomy 18:14). Since the Book of Genesis,

Identifying Demons

Satan has proposed to men to research the knowledge of hidden things (Genesis 3:4–7). The Bible said that hidden things belong to God: "The secret things belong unto the Lord our God: but those things which are revealed belong unto us and to our children for ever, that we may do all the words of this law" (Deuteronomy 29:29).

There are several ways divination is practiced:

- Astrology: a divinatory art based on observation of stars. Astrologists consult the stars to predict events and the destiny of people. The means of consulting is a horoscope (Deuteronomy 18:10).
- Cartomancy: predicting the future by interpretation of tarot cards. It is a game of cards marked with different images than an ordinary set of cards, whose mystery is explained by a secret doctrine reserved to those who have been initiated.
- Necromancy: when there is invocation of dead people by a bewitcher to know the future.
- "Juju" practice: The "juju' is an African cult close to voodoo. The "juju" man pretends to predict the future and reverse undesirable events. In fact, he sends curses on people.
- Chiromancy: a divinatory art that consists of predicting of the future or telling one's nature by reading lines in the palm of his hands. The person who practices chiromancy is called a fortuneteller (Deuteronomy 18:11).
- Telepathy: Telepathy is the transmission of thoughts not using sensorial means. The means of transportation is a satanic spirit.
- Spiritism: People who practice spiritism enter in contact with the dead and begin to have strange manifestations. Demonic spirits hide behind these

manifestations and take the names and the voices of these dead people and will sometimes reveal hidden things to the person who consults the spiritist.
- Acupuncture:[20] a medical treatment of Chinese origin consisting in planting silver or gold needles in certain nerves in the body (called vital lines of power). This method was discovered through radiasthesy, which pretends to be a medical science. The needles used are "blessed" by oriental masters.[21]
- Psychoanalysis (not to be mixed with psychiatry, which is the study and treatment of mental illnesses): a psychological investigation aiming to bring back unclear feelings to the consciousness of a person.

Today it is used to treat neurosis. It denies the reality of sin. It would, for example, justify the behavior of a pedophile by the fact that during his childhood he was victim of sexual abuses. They will try to bring back his memory as part of the therapy. What the psychoanalysis ignores is the fact that those abuses open doors to the unclean spirit in the life of the child. In adulthood those unclean spirits lead him to do the same thing. Therefore it is necessary to deal with those unclean spirits. In order to bring back the past of the patient, some psychoanalysts use occult methods such as hypnosis that open other doors to the unclean spirits. The hypnotist puts the patient into an artificial sleep by using demonic spirits that can easily enter into the patient's life.

When Christians are sick and have to go through medical techniques that will put them in an unconscious state, they have to claim the protection of the blood of Jesus.

---

[20] Derek Prince, *Blessing or Curse*, p.69.
[21] Rebecca Brown, *He came to set the captives free*, p.171.

Consequences of Satanic Actions in People's Lives

Even without getting a door or a tie to bind and destroy lives, satanic spirits take various actions to afflict people. These actions can affect unbelievers and Christians; satanic actions can also disturb flora and fauna; for example: some droughts, famines, wars, floods, and earthquakes. By means of prayers the effects of these actions can be reversed or neutralized regarding their consequences on Christians. Then it is not exaggerated the extent spiritual warfare for the deliverance of the Christian from negative effects of his environment. Neither is it exaggerated the events that can occur because of satanic works.

In conclusion, first, sin must be confessed and renounced. Renouncing sin cuts off Satan's legal right of action. Doors opened must be closed by special prayers: that is the deliverance operation. Also a Christian can fall back into spiritual bondage if he opens spiritual doors again.

Questionnaire

1. How can identifying demons help to cast them out?

   _____

   _____

2. What difference is there between symptoms and the actual presence of demons?

   _____

   _____

3. What are some of the behaviors that are symptomatic of demonic presence?

4. How can one be open to the Holy Spirit in order to receive His help?

5. What kind of attitude should Christians develop toward the kingdom of darkness in order to advance the kingdom of God?

6. From where do satanic demons operate now? How do they proceed to get doors opened?

7. What are the three modes of demonic operations?

Identifying Demons

8. How did God protect man from being bitten by the snake?

   _____

   _____

9. What are the two types of doors that the enemy can use?

   _____

   _____

10. According to Jeremiah 7:16–18, how did God express His anger against idolatry and particularly those who worship of the queen of heaven?

    _____

    _____

11. What are the consequences of satanic actions in people's lives?

    _____

    _____

Chapter Five

Casting Out Demons

Preparation for God's Intervention

Let the candidate understand that the Lord is willing and ready to deliver him (Psalm 9:9; Luke 4:18). Before casting out demons, some preparation is needed.

Preparation by Repenting

The candidate for deliverance must be taken through a process of preparation for God to intervene, because God said that there is a type of sorrow that leads to salvation (2 Corinthians 7:10).

The person who is suffering from oppression must be helped to see how much God loves him even though he has disappointed God. He must be brought to the point of understanding how much, through the cross and the blood of Christ, God has demonstrated His great unconditional love and how much, through disobedience to God and service to the devil, one has responded to God's love by hurting His heart.

This part of the preparation is responsible for producing in one's heart the sorrow of having hurt God by violating His commandments. If the person is truly sorrowful at this point, it will lead him to a real heart-turning from the sin and the devil and a coming back to God. The Bible promises that this kind of repentance will produce salvation (2 Corinthians 7:10).

This is critical in setting free those who are under demonic oppression. One must be led through these basic steps:

- acknowledge the wrong done to God
- be determined not to do it again
- ask for mercy and forgiveness from God
- ask for grace to enable him not to do it again

But first of all, one must be willing to let go of the hatred and bitterness of his/her heart, and forgive others. God will forgive as He also forgives those who have wronged Him.

The wrong done to God can be summarized as follows: idolatry, sexual immorality, witchcraft, evil altars, evil covenants, evil pacts and oaths, evil sacrifices, magic, divination, and sects.

Even though one may not have practiced these iniquities personally, nevertheless he must still ask forgiveness of God because the bloodline, generational iniquities, are passed on. The sin of Adam and Eve has been credited into the account of every man even though every man was not present at Eden. And man has to do something about it.

Preparation by Renouncing

The second aspect of preparation needed is obtained through renouncing. God said: "And have no fellowship with the unfruitful works of darkness, but rather reprove them" (Ephesians 5:11). After repenting, the next step is that one should throw out what was wrong: he must definitively renounce and reject these evil things because he no longer desires them in his life, because he no longer desires to have fellowship with the unfruitful works of darkness. There cannot be fellowship between light and darkness. There must be a clear line in one's life: one should not tolerate, no matter the pleasure or "benefit," darkness in his life. Therefore, one should be helped to choose light and reject darkness. This choice must be activated in a person's life by leading him to speaking directly to these evil things and rejecting them. This is one of the strongest ways of resisting the devil and making him flee (James 4:7).

Therefore the soul in need of deliverance must be wholeheartedly participating in speaking with conviction:

- He must be led to speak, renounce, and reject all the iniquities that he has practiced and those that have been practiced by his parents and ancestors: idolatry, sexual immorality, witchcraft, evil altars, evil covenants, evil pacts and oaths, evil sacrifices, magic, divination, and sects.
- He must also be led to speak to, renounce, and reject all evil spirits that are acting behind these iniquities: Satan, queen of heaven, spirit of death, spirit of infirmity, spirit of witchcraft, spirit of sickness, spirit of sexual immorality, incubus and succubus, and any other particular spirit that may have entered through these iniquities: spirit of idolatry, sexual immorality, witchcraft, evil altars, evil covenants, evil pacts and oaths, evil sacrifices, magic, divination, and sects.
- He must also renounce and reject all the works these evil spirits may have been doing in his life: oppression, obsession, possession, murder, wickedness,

infirmity, paralysis, sickness, disease, backwardness, failures, limitations, blockages, impossibilities, isolation, loneliness, fear, rejection, evil thoughts, lies, pride, foolishness, blasphemy, evil eye, deceit, malice, procrastination, compromise, memory loss, fantasizing, worry, restlessness, stealing, addictions, intoxication, abortions, miscarriages, and contamination.

- He must also renounce and reject all the negative habits and ways of speaking, thinking and acting: the renewing of the mind is absolutely necessary to effectively deal with the "house" of evil spirits: "When the unclean spirit is gone out of a man, he walketh through dry places, seeking rest; and finding none, he saith, I will return unto my house whence I came out" (Luke 11:24–26).

At this level in the process of deliverance, evil spirits may start manifesting and leaving. But it is important not to focus on and follow the manifestations of the demons. These can distract the whole process and make it less fruitful. It is also important not to make conversation with demons. The deliverance minister must only torment them with commandments, urge them to leave the oppressed person, keep on pressing on until they leave.

Preparation by Cleansing

The last aspect of the preparation is the cleansing: God promises that "if we walk in the light, as he is in the light, we have fellowship one with another, and the blood of Jesus Christ his Son cleanseth us from all sin.... If we confess our sins, he is faithful and just to forgive us our sins, and to cleanse us from all unrighteousness" (1 John 1:7, 9).

Therefore, the candidate must be led to believe and confess in line with God's promise of cleansing:

- He must be led to totally submit himself to the Lord Jesus: life, spirit, soul, body, family, relationships, and possessions.
- He must be led to reaffirm that he is a child of God, that he belongs to Jesus, that he is in the light, and that he is determined to walk in the light and bear witness to the light all the days of his life.
- He must be led to believe and confess that "God is full of compassion and gracious, longsuffering and plenteous in mercy and truth" (Psalm 86:15).
- He must be led to believe and confess that God is faithful to fulfill His Word, that God's Word will never return void unto Him, that God watches over His Word to perform it (Isaiah 55:11).
- He must be led to believe that God "is nigh unto all them that call upon him, to all that call upon Him in truth" (Psalm 145:18).
- Now, he must be led to ask God, on the basis of His promise, to cleanse him with the precious blood of Jesus.
- He must be allowed to also ask God, by himself, for cleansing with the blood of Jesus.
- He must believe that he has received what he has asked and start thanking God.

Execution of Deliverance

Then, we arrive at the execution of the deliverance itself. The body, with hands and feet, are the vehicle to carry out the commands of the Head (Jesus). If the body fails to enforce them, the commands remain dead letters: Here, it is the declarative mode that must be used to pronounce biblical truth and commandments.

Setting the Spiritual Atmosphere

    A. Exalting Jesus: Declaring His Lordship over the visible and the invisible: We must lift Him up above everything. We confess: "You are the Lord, You are the king, You are the ruler of the universe above the visible and the invisible, everything was made by You." By confessing that every knee shall bow before Him and declaring that today Jesus is here and every demon shall bow, we are exalting Him (Colossians 1:12–20).

    B. Taking authority and exercising it in the name of Jesus:

- We declare that he has given us authority to deal with them in His name (Mark 16:17).
- We forcefully declare that He gave us authority to tread on serpents and scorpions; that He said we shall cast out demons in His name (Mark 16:17); that He said He has all authority in heaven and earth (Matthew 28:18).
- We are operating in the authority that is contained in His name, the name above every name, the name that can bring salvation and deliverance, even now.
- We forcefully declare our authority: "Wherefore God also hath highly exalted him, and given him a name which is above every name: That at the name of Jesus every knee should bow, of things in heaven, and things in earth, and things under the earth...." (Philippians 2:9–11). "And what is the exceeding greatness of his power toward

us who believe, according to the working of his mighty power, Which he wrought in Christ, when he raised him from the dead, and set him at his own right hand in the heavenly places, Far above all principality, and power, and might, and dominion, and every name that is named, not only in this world, but also in that which is to come" (Ephesians 1:19–22). "And hath raised us up together, and made us sit together in heavenly places in Christ Jesus" (Ephesians 2:6).

C. Inviting the Holy Spirit and releasing His ministry: One of the most important aspects when it is time to pray for the deliverance of someone is to rely on the Holy Spirit, inviting Him to come and release His ministry. This is done through confessing the Word of God, confessing warfare prayer verses, and effectively taking authority. Matthew 12:28 says: "But if I cast out devils by the Spirit of God, then the kingdom of God is come unto you"—"by the Spirit of God," this is very important.

We must now concentrate on the Holy Spirit, believing He is going to do the work, inviting Him in and confessing every word that Jesus has given as a promise concerning the Holy Spirit. We must believe that He will cause His Word to be fire in our mouth, thank Him that His Word will not return to Him void, thank Him that He is going to use us like He used Jesus to do wonders.

D. Bringing demonic forces under the lordship of Jesus: We bring them by force under the lordship of Jesus Christ by telling the demonic forces that we bring them under the lordship of Jesus Christ. We declare it with persistent faith.

E. Commanding and releasing power to cast out demons: How do we do that? The declarations must be commands made directly to Satan and his demons.

- First, we destroy their grounds and power by issuing decrees of destruction, breaking, cutting off, rooting out, dismantling, crashing, pulling down (Exodus 34:13).
- Then, we start giving our commands (with authority) to demons to leave: "I command you in the name of Jesus: Go to dry places! Go and come no more! You have no choice! It's not an 'if,' not a choice, not a request, but it's a command! You demon of fornication, *go*! I cast you out of this body! This body is the temple of the Holy Spirit! You cannot stay in this temple! Jesus has sent us to cast you out! And we cast you out! *Now!* In Jesus' name, *Out*! You are leaving! Go to the dry places! *Now!* In Jesus' mighty name! The Bible says with all authority and power we command and even the unclean spirits obey: 'And the seventy returned again with joy, saying, "Lord, even the devils are subject unto us through thy name"' (Luke10:17). So it is right now! Jesus said in His name we cast out demons! Now, in Jesus' name, *go*!" We continue harassing the demons until they are gone.
- During the prayer there may be manifestations and these manifestations can come in various ways. Once we finish praying, we will perceive the change. When the change comes, the person will express a great joy and will start saying

things such as "I feel as if…" You will know that something has happened. When you ask the person if he loves Jesus, he will start smiling and praising God, and the whole team will praise God together.

Part 3
Counseling Post-deliverance

We have seen that deliverance ministry has a place and must have its place in the Church. A Christian always needs deliverance. After deliverance, he must continually renew his mind and periodically do self-deliverance.

Chapter Six

THE RENEWAL OF THE MIND

Deliverance can help to free a person in case of demonic oppression. But in order to retain the fruit of deliverance and continue to increase, one must work diligently to renew his mind. Renewing of the mind is absolutely necessary for all of God's children. Deliverance helps, or facilitates, the process of renewing the mind in case of demonic oppression. Therefore, Christians should never think that deliverance can solve all their spiritual problems: there is a necessity to take responsibility to grow.

As stated before, deliverance is in three tenses: past, present, and future. After the present deliverance, the next step is the "future" deliverance. That is possible only through the renewing of the mind. It is crucial that Christians who have benefited from a deliverance process take immediately personal responsibility to discipline their own lives (Luke 9:23).

    A. They should seek to feed their spirit with the Word of God that they might become strong in subduing soul and body to their regenerated spirit. This is done by building upon the sayings of Jesus.

- First step of building: Jesus said: "Go and sin no more" (John 8:11). Jesus is indicating that it is a personal decision and an act of the will. It is possible because Jesus said it. Everyone who gets delivered must endeavor not to go back to sinning, but he must adopt the lifestyle of practical righteousness.
- Second step of building: "I will liken him unto a wise man, which built his house upon a rock...." (Matthew 7:24–27). Building must be upon the Rock of the Word to be able to withstand the rain, the floods, and the winds. Jesus qualifies those who build that way as being wise.
- Third step of building: "behold, there went out a sower to sow..." (Mark 4:3–20). Sowing the Word of God in the heart is a key in building a strong spiritual life. Sowing is the one main factor that determines the future and the fruit of one's life. "Thy word, have I hid in mine heart, that I might not sin against thee" (Psalm119:11).
- Fourth step of building: "Therefore take no thought, saying..." (Matthew 6:31). Jesus said that "saying" is the means by which "sowing" is done. You sow the Word in your mind and end up producing fruits.

B. The person who receives deliverance should also seek the fruits of the Spirit by giving himself to obedience and submission to the Holy Spirit through:

- doing the Word
- being prayerful
- have a habit of fasting
- fellowshipping
- serving at home and in the church
- witnessing

Self-Deliverance After Deliverance

- Jesus warns us that once the demons are cast out they try to come back and take back what they have lost. Self-deliverance is a means to stop this possible return and to allow the continuation of the renewing of the mind. Therefore, self-deliverance helps to keep the fruits of deliverance and to grow in freedom.
- Self-deliverance is a part of the Christian's spiritual discipline. Many Christians neglect or ignore it. Therefore they suffer uselessly from the negative consequences of their carelessness and ignorance.
- It includes the steps of deliverance such as repentance, renouncement, purification, and warfare prayer. Yet at this point, in terms of repentance, it is not necessary to go back to the generational iniquities.

Conclusion

Deliverance must be taught in the Church of our Lord Jesus Christ. Its biblical foundation and process must be understood and mastered by the Church. God is searching for ministers who will give themselves to Him and pay the price in the Word of God and in prayer and fasting for the anointing to meet the needs of the people and set them free from satanic oppression. Like He did through Jesus, the

Holy Spirit is working in the character of yielded vessels and also giving them ability to expose and defeat the enemy, destroying his works more than ever before.

The light of the glorious gospel of our Lord Jesus is shining, and the awareness of the devices of the devil is increasing. Evermore captives and oppressed are being delivered and healed. That is God's desire for every Christian: to get equipped, and by getting in the flow of the Spirit be used to bring deliverance to the captives (Matthew 12:28).

With the institution of the ministry of deliverance in the local church, the effectiveness of the Church will be increased. Deliverance ministry must move from an informal to a structured ministry organized to provide a systematic service to the body of Christ.

We have herein exposed our thoughts to help to understand, establish, and develop the ministry of deliverance in the local church or a small group and to equip the deliverance minister. Our personal experience of this has proven that the spiritual growth of the local church and the process of discipleship benefit from such organization of the ministry of deliverance. We pray that this book will help the local church to establish the ministry of deliverance and help as a guideline for the development of the character requirements and the equipment and training necessary for the minister of deliverance to operate with excellence.

Questionnaire

1. What discipline is recommended after the deliverance of a Christian?

   _____

   _____

The Renewal of the Mind

2. How is one to proceed for the renewal of the mind?

3. How is one to proceed for self-deliverance?

Appendix 1

Four-Step Session for Deliverance

Step 1: Repentance from Iniquities

    A. Ask forgiveness for (names of people to be forgiven):

- hatred
- bitterness
- unforgiveness

    B. Ask forgiveness to God for these personal and generational iniquities:

- idolatry
- sexual immorality
- witchcraft
- sacrifices
- covenants
- pacts
- oaths

- magic
- divination
- initiation into sects

Step 2: Renouncement

   A. Iniquities

- Idolatry and all spirits that enter through that door
- Sexual sin and all spirits that enter through that door
- Witchcraft and all spirits that enter through that door

   B. Evil spirits

- Satan and all satanic spirits
- Death and spirit of death
- Infirmity and all spirits that enter through that door
- Queen of heaven and all spirits that enter through that door
- Husband of night and all spirits that enter through that door
- Wife of night and all spirits that enter through that door, etc.

   C. Works

- Oppression and the spirit of oppression
- Fear and the spirit of fear
- Rejection and the spirit of rejection
- Procrastination and the spirit of procrastination
- Obsession and the spirit of obsession

Appendix 1: Four-Step Session for Deliverance

- Possession and the spirit of possession
- Infirmity and the spirit of infirmity
- Backwardness and the spirit of backwardness
- Limitation and the spirit of limitation
- Compromise and the spirit of compromise
- Memory loss and the spirit of loss of memory
- Fantasizing and the spirit of fantasizing
- Worry and the spirit of worry
- Restlessness and the spirit of restlessness
- Addiction and the spirit of addiction, etc.

Step 3: Cleansing with the Blood of Jesus

A. Determine to walk in the light
B. Ask God to cleanse you with the blood of Jesus
C. Submit to the Lordship of Jesus

Step 4: Prayer of Authority (Warfare Aiming at Breakthrough in Delivering the Oppressed)

End the session with praise, thanksgiving, and giving all glory to God.

Appendix 2

Deliverance Prayer to Set the Oppressed Free

Preparation of Spiritual Atmosphere

- A. As stated before, the deliverance session starts with an opening prayer. The deliverance captain (or leader) will lead the deliverance session.
- B. The spiritual atmosphere must be transformed to allow an effective deliverance to take place. Jesus is the One who performs the deliverance (Hebrews 2:15). Therefore, we need to call for His presence and create an atmosphere where He is exalted and reigns.
- C. One of the best ways to bring about the manifest presence of God is to praise and worship Him from the heart using the Word of God to express our love and gratitude for having Him as our Father. Such atmosphere terrorizes unclean spirits.
- D. The oppressed person should be led through the steps for deliverance and be prayed for.

Deliverance Prayer

   A. Repentance and forgiveness

Father God, I forgive everyone (call them by name) that has hurt me. I release them in the name of Jesus.

Father God, I come before Your throne of grace and I ask You to also forgive me for the iniquities of my parents, my grandparents, my great-grandparents and my great-great-grandparents (Exodus 20:5).

Forgive me for their iniquities such as hatred, bitterness, jealousy, anger, envy, unforgiveness, murder, sexual immorality, witchcraft, sorcery, magic, idolatry, divination, division, heresies, and initiation into sects.

Forgive me for the altars, covenants, oaths, pacts, and/or sacrifices they made to Satan consciously or unconsciously.

I repent for all their iniquities known or unknown and ask You, Father, to cleanse me from anything that afflicted me because of their iniquities.

Father God, I repent for the sins I have committed such as hatred, bitterness, jealousy, anger, envy, unforgiveness, murder, sexual immorality, witchcraft, sorcery, magic, idolatry, divination, division, heresies, or initiation into sects.

Forgive me for the altars, covenants, oaths, pacts, and sacrifices that I made to Satan consciously or unconsciously.

APPENDIX 2: DELIVERANCE PRAYER TO SET THE OPPRESSED FREE

I repent of all my sins known or unknown and ask You, Father, to cleanse me from anything that afflicted me because of my own sins (confess sins specifically one by one).

B. Renouncement (Proverbs 28:13)

I renounce Satan and all his demons, in the name of Jesus.

I renounce all ancestral altars and/or covenants made by me or on my behalf in the name of Jesus.

I renounce all the demons that came into my life because of sacrifices, altars, covenants, oaths, or pacts made by me or by my ancestors consciously or unconsciously.

I renounce all curses and all demons enforcing those curses, in Jesus' name.

I renounce the spirit of witchcraft, voodoo, sorcery, magic, divination, idolatry, mermaid, queen of heaven, leviathan, illuminati, fornication, adultery, oral sex, sodomy, orgy, pornography, death, poverty, failure, infirmity, sickness, slavery, spiritual husband, spiritual wife, evil spiritual marriage (and so on), in the name of Jesus.

I renounce any evil covenant made through illegal sexual relations, in the name of Jesus.

I renounce and break all evil soul ties made with former sexual partners, in Jesus' name.

C. Prayer of Authority and Command

O Jehovah, Lord of hosts, Father of Glory, I call upon You, the Mighty Warrior, and I exalt You. I lift You up in this place and in the life of Your child. Hallowed be Thy name.

Lord Jesus, all the authority in heaven and earth has been given to You. Lord, release Your power in this place, that the powers of darkness might be destroyed, and that Your Name be glorified.

By the authority of the Lord Jesus, I disrupt and cut every evil communication between this place and the kingdom of darkness.

I bind Satan and all the demons, principalities, powers, rulers of darkness of this world, and the spiritual wickedness in heavenly places operating against us in the name of Jesus of Nazareth, the Son of God (Matthew 18:18).

I paralyze all demons sent to rescue and replace the ones cast out and resist this deliverance in the name of Jesus Christ of Nazareth.

I saturate this place with the blood of the Lord Jesus (Revelation 12:11).

Holy Ghost, I invite You and ask You to take control of this deliverance.

I forbid any evil spirit to harm (X) before leaving his body, in the name of Jesus.

I bind the master evil spirit, in the name of Jesus.

I send the blood of Jesus against you to torment you and to render you powerless, in Jesus' name.

Appendix 2: Deliverance Prayer to Set the Oppressed Free

I cast you out, you Satan, queen of heaven, spirit of witchcraft, magic, idolatry, sexual immorality, etc. I command you to go to the dry places.

I cast you out and forbid you from coming back again.

I break the curse of witchcraft, magic, poverty, failure, divorce, etc., in the name of Jesus (Galatians 3:13).

I close all doors the demons used to enter in (X)'s life in the name of Jesus.

I claim back any blessing that has been stolen from (X)'s life, in Jesus' name.

Closing Prayer

After the deliverance session, the deliverance captain must ask the formerly oppressed person to thank the Lord.

After release, the whole group must praise the Lord for having delivered (X). Then the captain will close the session with prayer.

I thank You, Lord Jesus, because You are faithful. Lord, restore everything the devil has destroyed in (X)'s life, in the name of Jesus. Father, be thou glorified in (X)'s life, in Jesus' name.

Appendix 3

Prayer to Bring Healing to the Sick

Begin with the Blood of Jesus

   A. Start with praise: sing songs of the blood of Jesus

   B. Pray

     Father, I ask Your mercy on behalf of (X) and family, in Jesus' name.

     I ask that You forgive his sins because of Your mercy and love and because of the blood that Jesus shed on the cross for him.

     Father, thank You for Your mercy, which allowed Jesus to shed His blood for the reconciliation of (X) with You.

     Father, thank You for Your mercy, which allowed Jesus to shed His blood for (X) to have peace with You.

     Father, thank You for Your mercy, which allowed Jesus to shed His blood for the justification of (X).

Loose Him and Let Him Go!

Father, thank You for Your mercy, which allowed Jesus to shed His blood to give victory to (X).

Father, thank You for Your mercy, which allowed Jesus to shed His blood for the redemption of (X).

Father, let the blood of Jesus wash (X) from all his sins.

Father, thank You that Jesus was despised and rejected for (X).

Thank You that Jesus took the pains, grief, and sorrows of (X).

Thank You that Jesus was stricken and smitten for (X).

Thank You that Jesus was afflicted for (X).

Thank You that Jesus was wounded for the transgressions of (X).

Thank You that Jesus was bruised for the iniquities of (X).

Thank You that Jesus was chastised for the peace of (X).

Thank You that with the stripes of Jesus, (X) is healed.

Thank You, Father, that because of the blood of Jesus, the life of (X) will manifest the destruction of Satan.

Thank You, Father, that because of the blood of Jesus, the life of (X) will manifest the destruction of the law of sin and death.

APPENDIX 3: PRAYER TO BRING HEALING TO THE SICK

Thank You, Father, that because of the blood of Jesus, the life of (X) will manifest the defeat of the forces of darkness.

Thank You, Father, that because of the blood of Jesus, the life of (X) will manifest the destruction of ordinances and handwritings contrary to (X).

Thank You, Father, that because of the blood of Jesus, the life of (X) will manifest the destruction of works of the devil: sicknesses, diseases, oppression.

Thank You, Father, that because of the blood of Jesus, the life of (X) will manifest the victory of the cross.

Father, I thank You that the blood of Jesus is flowing through the body of (X) and bringing healing and abundant life.

Continue by Praying for the Intervention of the Holy Spirit

A. Praises again: sing songs of the Holy Spirit
B. Acknowledge the Holy Spirit as God
C. Submit to Him and what He is doing
D. Ask the Holy Spirit to come and overtake the life and the special circumstances through which (X) is going.
E. Ask the manifestation of the power of the Holy Spirit in the body of (X).
F. Proclaim that the Holy Spirit is quickening (X)'s body and infusing healing, life, and strength into every cell of his body.
G. Declare Jesus Lord in the life and every part of the body of (X), lift Him up, and proclaim that every knee must bow to Jesus including sicknesses.

H. Declare that Jesus Christ is God and He must be exalted in (X)'s life and God glorified.

Continue Praying to Cast Out Evil Spirits and Heal Sicknesses

A. Sing songs of praises and worship exalting Jesus and glorifying God.
B. Proclaim the Word of God (take a specific verse), which will not return void from (X)'s life unto God.
C. Reject and nullify any negative word spoken over (X).
D. Prophesy over (X)'s life concerning the work of God and the future of (X) and his testimony that it will glorify God.
E. Take authority over every evil spirit and its works and cast them out of (X)'s life.
F. Thank God for doing all that we have asked, and seal all the answers with the blood of Jesus.

Appendix 4

Activating Covenant Prayer

A. Thank You, Jesus, for You have become my Jehovah Jireh; for it is written: "God shall supply all my need according to His riches in glory by Christ Jesus" (Philippians 4:19).
B. Thank You, Jesus, for You have become my Jehovah Rapha; for it is written: "Who His own self bare our sins in His own body on the tree, that we, being dead to sin, should live unto righteousness: by whose stripes we were healed" (1 Peter 2:24).
C. Thank You, Jesus, for You have become my Jehovah Nissi; for it is written: "When He putteth forth His own sheep, He goeth before them, and the sheep follow Him: for they know His voice" (John 10:4).
D. Thank You, Jesus, for You have become my Jehovah M'Kaddesh; for it is written: "But of Him are ye in Christ Jesus, who of God is made unto us wisdom, righteousness, and sanctification, and redemption" (1 Corinthians 1:30).

E. Thank You, Jesus, for You have become my Jehovah Shalom; for it is written: "For He is our peace, who hath made both one, and hath broken down the middle wall of partition between us" (Ephesians 2:14).
F. Thank You, Jesus, for You have become my Jehovah Rohe; for it is written: "I am the Good Shepherd: the Good Shepherd giveth His life for the sheep" (John 10:11).
G. Thank You, Jesus, for You have become my Jehovah Tsidkenu; for it is written: "And be found in Him, not having my own righteousness, which is of the law, but that which is through the faith of Christ, the righteousness which is of God by faith" Philippians 3:9. "For He (God) hath made Him to be sin for us, who knew no sin, that we might be the righteousness of God in Him" (2 Corinthians 5:21).
H. Thank You, Jesus, for You have become my Jehovah Shammah; for it is written: "All authority in heaven and in earth has been given to me. Therefore go and make disciples of all nations, baptizing them in the name of the Father and of the Son and of the Holy Spirit, teaching them to observe all things whatsoever I have commanded you. And, lo, I am with you always, even unto the end of the world" (Matthew 28:18–20, NKJV). I thank You, Jesus, my Lord and my God.

… Appendix 5

Soul Diagnosis Form

1. Personal salvation experience and spiritual covering:

   _____

   _____

2. Name meaning (if any):

   _____

   _____

3. Previous history of marriage/divorce:

   _____

   _____

4. Are you born again? *Yes/No* When?

   _____

   _____

Loose Him and Let Him Go!

5. If you were to die today, do you know where you would spend eternity?

   _____

   _____

6. Suppose you were to die today, appear before God in heaven, and He asks you "By what right should I allow you into My presence?" How would you answer Him?

   _____

   _____

7. First John 5:11–12 says: "God has given us eternal life and this life is in His Son. He who has the Son has the life he who doesn't have the Son of God doesn't have the life." Do you have the Son of God in you (2 Corinthians 13:5)?

   _____

   _____

8. How do you know that you have received Him? 1) The Word of God said so for those who accept Him as Lord and Savior, 2) you have the fruits of the life of the Son (fruits of the Holy Spirit), 3) the Spirit Himself testifies to our spirits.

   _____

   _____

APPENDIX 5: SOUL DIAGNOSIS FORM

9. Are you plagued with doubts concerning your salvation? Please explain:

_____

_____

10. Are you presently enjoying fellowship with other believers, and if so where and when?

_____

_____

Family-Level Doorways and Generational Curses (Exodus 20:3–5)

Religions

11. To your knowledge, have any of your parents, grandparents, or great-grandparents ever been involved in any occultism, cults, or non-Christian religious practices? Please describe:

_____

_____

_____

_____

12. Briefly describe your parents' Christian experience:

_____

_____

_____

Loose Him and Let Him Go!

Marital Status, Relationships, and Sexuality

13. Marriages and divorces history in your family:

   _____
   _____
   _____
   _____

14. Was your father clearly the head of the home? How? Was there a reversal of roles where your mother ruled the home?

   _____
   _____
   _____
   _____

15. How did your parents treat each other?

   _____
   _____
   _____
   _____

16. Was there an adulterous affair to your knowledge involving your parents or grandparents? Any incestuous relationships?

   _____
   _____

APPENDIX 5: SOUL DIAGNOSIS FORM

17. Are you adopted or did foster parents or legal guardians raise you?

18. Describe the emotional atmosphere in your home while you were growing up. Describe your relationship to your parents.

Health

19. Are there any addictive problems in your family history?

20. Is there a history of mental illness? Please describe:

21. Please indicate if you have any history of the following ailments in your family:

    - tuberculosis
    - cancer
    - heart disease
    - ulcers
    - diabetes
    - blood disease
    - other

22. Please indicate any problem with pregnancy, barrenness, child-bearing, and miscarriages in your family:

    _____
    _____
    _____
    _____

23. Have you participated in or done any sacrifice of rituals? If so, explain:

    _____
    _____
    _____
    _____

APPENDIX 5: SOUL DIAGNOSIS FORM

24. Was there any incision done on your body?

    _____

    _____

25. Were you dedicated to any family god?

    _____

    _____

26. Have you ever joined any fraternity (sorority, Rosicrucians, freemasonry, New Age), participated in transcendental meditation, yoga, cultural dances, masquerades or other forms of idol worship, palm reading, white magic, horoscope, astrology, fortune telling, Ouija board games?

    _____

    _____

27. Have you been involved in any sects?

    _____

    _____

28. Have you ever used (or still use) charms, blessed pictures, incense, candlesticks, waist beads, protection rings, dedicated perfumes, soaps, creams, bath/body oils?

    _____

    _____

29. Do you know of any curse covenant in your life (or family)?

30. Do you know of any contributory story about your conception, birth, and childhood?

31. Have you ever visited shrines (rooms dedicated to other gods)?

32. Do you feel you have inherited specific curses from your family (divorce, barrenness, bad luck, rejection)?

33. Is there a history of violence in your family, violent death (murder, suicide, accidents, or burglaries/thefts conducive to murder)?

APPENDIX 5: SOUL DIAGNOSIS FORM

34. Visual: Do you see things that other people present with you cannot see?

   _____

   _____

35. Audio: Do you hear voices?

   _____

   _____

36. Olfactory: Do you smell odors others do not smell? Foul odors? Perfume?

   _____

   _____

37. Déjà vu: Do you experience things in your dreams before they manifest in the reality?

   _____

   _____

38. Clairvoyance: Do you have the power to predict things?

   _____

   _____

39. Do you lose things: personal effects, money?

   _____

   _____

Loose Him and Let Him Go!

40. Do you forget easily? Are you lazy?

   _____

   _____

41. Do you procrastinate, waiting until the last minute to do things that need to be done?

   _____

   _____

42. Do you wear jewelry: rings, necklaces, or clothing that you do not know where and how you got them?

   _____

   _____

43. Have you lost your engagement ring or wedding ring strangely?

   _____

   _____

44. Is there a story of miscarriage or abortion in your life (either physical or spiritual—whenever something good is about to happen it "fades away")?

   _____

   _____

APPENDIX 5: SOUL DIAGNOSIS FORM

45. Have you had any strange experiences?

    _____

    _____

46. Are you excessively stubborn? Do you blow up? Are you callous (enjoy seeing others suffer)?

    _____

    _____

47. Are you restless? Addicted (alcohol, sex, music, tobacco, drugs)?

    _____

    _____

48. Do you have sleepless nights (nightmares, recurrent dreams, sweats)?

    _____

    _____

49. How is your menstrual cycle? Are you still menstruating? Did you experience early menopause? Are you having extreme menstrual pains?

    _____

    _____

50. Do you scratch your body or fidget unnaturally?

    _____

51. Do you experience dizziness often?

52. Has your sickness defied medical therapy?

53. Are you unable to maintain any lasting relationships with the opposite sex?

54. Are you unable to give birth normally without any medical explanation?

55. Are you suffering from unaccountable leanness in spite of heavy eating?

56. Are you proud, boastful?

57. Do you have backwardness in your life's pursuit?

58. Do you get sad and moody without cause?

59. Are you easily irritated?

APPENDIX 5: SOUL DIAGNOSIS FORM

60. Are you afraid of mixing with people; hence, always wanting to be alone?

61. Are there unnatural feelings of heat or movement in your body?

62. Do you have discussions with strong voices from within you?

63. Do you sense an invisible presence around you especially when you are alone (at night)?

64. Do you have excessive anger, hatred, bitterness, and jealousy?

65. Do you have unforgiveness? Against who?

66. Do you have excessive fear of water (rivers), snakes, insects, heights, and darkness?

67. Excessive sexual desire?

68. Indiscriminate sexual exposure?

   _____

69. Repressed sexual exposure?

   _____

70. Have you ever engaged in or are still engaged in:

   - masturbation
   - homosexuality
   - sodomy
   - lesbianism
   - bestiality
   - oral sex
   - fornication or adultery
   - incest
   - orgy

71. Do you feel:

   - rejected
   - confused
   - superior
   - inferior
   - insecure
   - self-pity, depressed

71. Do you like to cry? To weep?

   _____

APPENDIX 5: SOUL DIAGNOSIS FORM

72. Do you think of dying or committing suicide? Do you have recurrent dreams in which you die?

73. Do you worry unnecessarily over situations?

74. Do you want something and at the same time you don't want it (double-minded, undecided, wavering)?

75. Do you often:

- compromise
- doubt
- lose your memory
- procrastinate
- daydream
- fantasize
- lie
- criticize others
- mock others
- gossip
- curse others (even your children)

Loose Him and Let Him Go!

Dream State

    76. Do you forget your dreams often? Have nightmares where you are pursued by masquerades, madmen, animals, snakes, others?

Do you experience:

    77. Always climbing staircase without getting to the top?

    78. Falling from a cliff or high mountain into a bottomless ditch?

    79. Finding yourself in your secondary school uniform or dormitory?

    80. Writing an examination/passing an exam?

    81. Climbing a high hill?

    82. Wandering in the forest?

APPENDIX 5: SOUL DIAGNOSIS FORM

83. Fighting with animals?

84. Attending regular meetings?

85. Do you feel like you are being pressed down while asleep, unable to move or scream?

86. Do you go to specific markets in your dreams?

87. Do you feel strangled?

88. Do you receive gifts that sometimes manifest physically?

89. Do you wake up in the morning with incisions on your body? Do you feel tired after sleeping?

90. Do you attend weddings or are you married in your dreams?

91. Do you see yourself pregnant, carrying babies, having other children?

　　_____

Recommendations for Preparation before Deliverance Session

1. _____
　_____
　_____

2. _____
　_____
　_____

3. _____
　_____
　_____

Appendix 6

Hebrew/Greek Terms Translated by the English Verb Deliver

Hebrew *Yasha* (Judges 10:13): properly to be open, wide or free, by implication to be safe, causatively to free or succor, avenging, defend, deliver, help, preserve, rescue, be safe, bring salvation, save, get victory.

Hebrew *shaphat* (1 Samuel 24:15): to judge, by implication to vindicate or punish, plead, reason.

Hebrew *chalats* (Psalm 6:4, 50:15, 91:15, 119:153, 140:1): pull off, strip, depart, by implication deliver, draw out, loose, take away, withdraw self.

Hebrew *palat* (Psalm 17:13, 22:4, 8, 31:1, 37:40, 43:1, 71:4, 82:4, 91:14; Micah 6:14): slip out, escape, causatively deliver, carry away safe.

Hebrew *shub* (Genesis 27:32): relieve, retrieve, withdraw.

Hebrew *padah* (Psalm 69:18, 119:134): sever that is to ransom, release, preserve, redeem, rescue.

Hebrew *natah* (Job 36:18): stretch.

Hebrew *pada* (Job 33:24): retrieve.

Hebrew *parak* (Lamentations 5:8): break off, redeem.

Hebrew *shzab* (Daniel 3:15, 17, 6:14): leave, causatively free.

Hebrew *magan* (Hosea 11:8): shield, encompass with, figuratively rescue, hand safely over.

Hebrew *malat* (Job 6:23, 22:30; Psalm 33:17, 89:48, 116:4; Isaiah 46:2, 4; Jeremiah 39:18, 51:6, 45; Ezekiel 33:5; Amos 2:14, 15; Zechariah 2:7): properly to be smooth, by implication to escape as if by slipperiness, causatively to release or rescue, specifically to bring forth young, deliver (self), leap out, let alone, let go, preserve, save.

Hebrew *gaal* (Psalm 119:154): redeem (oriental law of kinship), to buy back a relative's property, perform the part of near, purchase, revenger.

Greek *rhuomai* (Matthew 6:13, 27:43; Luke 11:4; Romans 7:24; 2 Corinthians 1:10; 2 Timothy 4:18; 2 Peter 2:9): rush or draw for oneself, rescue.

Greek *didomi* (Acts 7:25): bring forth.

Greek *exaireo* (Acts 7:34; Galatians 1:4): tear out, select, figuratively release, pluck out, rescue.

Greek *charizomai* (Acts 25:11): favor, pardon, rescue, forgive, grant.

Greek *appallazzo* (Hebrews 2:15): change away, release, remove, depart.

Appendix 7

BIBLIOGRAPHY

Swope, M. R. *The Roots and Fruits of Fasting.* Illinois Wheaton: Tyndale House Publishers, (1998).

Mylander, C. and N. T. Anderson. *Setting Your Church Free.* California: Regal Books, (1994).

Anderson, N. *Victory Over the Darkness: Realizing the Power of Identity in Christ.* California: Regal Books, (1990).

Kraft, C. *I Give You Authority.* Michigan: Chosen Books, (2000).

Prince, D. *They Shall Expel Demons.* Michigan: Chosen Books, (2003).

Horrobin, P. *Healing Through Deliverance: The Biblical Basis.* England: Clays Ltd, (1994).

Eckhardt, J. *Belial the Wicked Ruler.* Chicago: Crusaders Ministries, (1998).

Dompreh, D. *The Roadmap to Abundant Life In Jesus Christ.* Indiana: AuthorHouse, (2003).

Olukoya, D. K. *Violent Prayers to Disgrace Stubborn Problems.* Nigeria: The Battle Cry Christian Ministries, (1999).

Sumrall, L. *Alien Entities: Beings From Beyond.* Indiana: LeSEA, (1984).

Greenwald, G. L. *Seductions Exposed: The Spiritual Dynamics Of Relationships.* California: Eagle's Nest, (1996).

Reynolds, Y. *The Dangers of Fornication.* New York: Revival Time Ministry, (2000).

Cookey, S. A. *Winning Your Battles before They Manifest.* Nigeria: Life-Gate, (1997).

Francis, R. *Counseling and Deliverance.* Benin City: Glorious Life, ().

Hammond, F. D. *Soul Ties.* Texas: The Children's Bread Ministry, (1988).

Frangipane, F. *The House Of The Lord: God's Plan to Liberate Your City from Darkness.* Florida: Creation House, (1991).

Prince, D. *Blessing Or Curse You Choose.* Michigan: Chosen Books, (1990).

Olukoya, D. K. *Release From Destructive Covenants.* Nigeria: Mountain Of Fire and Miracles Ministries, (1997).

Mwanaliti, S. *Deliverance for the Delivered.* Chicago: Crusaders Ministries, (2001).

Burns, C. *Masonic and Occult Symbols Illustrated.* Pennsylvania: Sharing, (1999).

Shelley, B.L. *Church History in the Plain Language.* Texas: Word, (1995).

Rallo, V. *Breaking Generational Curses and Pulling Down Strongholds.* Florida: Creation House Press, (2000).

Dickason, C. F. *Demon Possession and the Christian.* Illinois: Crossway Books (1987).

Mbadu, L. 666: *Au Centre d'un Nouveau Système Economique Mondial.* Belgium: TDS Editions, (2000).

Wigglesworth, S. *Anointing.* Pennsylvania: Whitaker House, (1999).

APPENDIX 7: BIBLIOGRAPHY

Wagner, C. P. *Breaking Strongholds in Your City*. California: Regal Books, (1993).
Schaeffer, F. A. *The Great Evangelical Disaster*. Illinois: Crossway Books, (1995).

Pleasant Word

To order additional copies of this title call:
1-877-421-READ (7323)
or please visit our web site at
www.pleasantwordbooks.com

If you enjoyed this quality custom published book,
drop by our web site for more books and information.

www.winepressgroup.com
"Your partner in custom publishing."